C016226985

REF

DEPARTMENT OF HEALTH

The Children Act 1989 Guidance and Regulations

Volume 10

Index

A NEW FRAMEWORK FOR THE CARE
AND UPBRINGING OF CHILDREN

LONDON: HMSO

© Crown copyright 1992
Applications for reproduction should be made to HMSO
First published 1992

ISBN 0 11 321538 X

CHILDREN ACT (1989) GUIDANCE AND REGULATIONS – INDEX

DURHAM COUNTY COUNCIL
Cultural Services

6226985

362.7

b – page number prefixes:
'V' refers to volume number
'CP' refers to *Patterns and Outcomes in Child Placement*
'PP' refers to *Principles and Practice in Regulations and Guidance*
'WT' refers to *Working Together under the Children Act*

A

abduction, V1.10, V1.16–17
  exemption from prosecution, V4.130
abduction of children in care, V1.64
  Part V of Act, WT.82–4
absconding, V4.123
  from local authority accomodation, V1.77
  secure accomodation, V1.66
absence without authority from children's
  home, V4.30
abuse, V4.30
  alertness to signs, WT.27
  at independent boarding schools, V5.6–7
  bizarre behaviour, WT.38
  by children or young people, WT.37,
    V4.33–4
  by staff, V4.34–5
  by stranger, WT.36–7
  by visitors to residential places, WT.34
  case conference, V3.53
  categories for registration, WT.48–9
  in children's homes, V4.32–5
  confidentiality, V4.33
  criminal investigations, WT.16, WT.17
  educational establishments' roles in
    prevention, WT.22
  entitlement to protection from, PP.7
  extra-familial, WT.36
  handling of allegations, V5.6
  inter-agency protection work, WT.5
  investigation, WT.9–10
  liaison of educational establishments with
    SSDs, WT.21
  local authority powers of investigation, V1.44
  management information, WT.113
  organised, WT.38–9
  physical, CP.34
  procedural guidance to staff, V4.33
  relationship between parents and baby,
    WT.18
  in residential settings, WT.34–6
  ritualised behaviour, WT.38
  scrutiny of progress of protection work, WT.6
  sharing information between agencies,
    WT.17
  staff training, V4.35
  see also sexual abuse
abused young people, sex education, V4.107
abusers, adult
  distinctions, WT.38
  work with, WT.37–8
academic potential, V3.105
  of young people being cared for, V4.115
access
  and local authority, V1.63
  termination, CP.45
  transitional arrangements for children in
    care, V1.79–80, V7.37
access disputes, CP.26, CP.42
  changes in thinking, CP.45–6
  local authority actions, CP.61–2
  parents and social workers, CP.45

Access to Health Records Act (1990), WT.11
Access to Personal Files Act (1987), WT.11
accomodation, WT.117, V1.63
  access for care leavers, CP.11–12
  admission to, CP.60
  for adults deemed to be risk to child, V2.20
  agreement of arrangements, V2.20–2
  by health and education authorities, V4.36–7
  by voluntary organisations, V5.17
  care leavers, CP.34
  for children in need, V2.8
  in children's homes, V4.12, V4.13–14
  emergency by police, WT.78–9
  in family centres, V2.19
  family links, V2.22
  financial assistance from local authority,
    V3.101
  halfway, V3.104
  in homes governed by Registered Homes
    Act (1984), V4.36–7
  in independent boarding schools, V5.4,
    V5.8–9
  juveniles absconding from, V1.77
  options, V2.21
  protection of children in, WT.33
  provision, CP.21, V2.20–2
  provision by local authority, WT.64, V1.76,
    V4.113–14
  and respite care, CP.48
  restriction of liberty, V4.18–19
  sheltered, V3.104
  for single homeless people, V3.103
  vetting, V4.8
  voluntary arrangements, V2.20–1
  voluntary sector aftercare services, V3.102
  for young people aged 16–20, V3.1–4
  see also secure accomodation
Accomodation of Children (Charge and
  Control) Regulations (1988), V3.28
accreditation systems, independent boarding
  schools, V5.3
adaptability, adult assumptions about children,
  CP.70, CP.71
adjournments, V1.27
  interim orders, V1.30
  secure accomodation, V4.127
adopted people
  legal rights over eighteen, V9.54
  legal rights in UK, V9.65
adopters, V9.6
  advice and information about allowances,
    V9.14
  annual statement of circumstances, V9.16
  changes in circumstances, V9.11
  financial resources, V9.12–13
  information on allowances, V9.10–11
  notification of allowance, V9.15–16
adoption
  access to birth records, V9.19–21
  certificate, V9.78
  Child Benefit, V9.8
  child's need for security and permanence,
    V9.10

  classification, CP.59
  definitions, V9.6–7
  family proceedings, V9.2
  and fostering, V3.29, V9.8
  freeing child for, V9.3
  harmonisation of law, V9.2–3
  intercountry, V8.40
  law changes, V9.1–4
  links with birth families, CP.24
  of older children, CP.55–6
  orders made by court, V9.2
  outcome, CP.67–8
  panel, V9.6
  parental responsibility, V9.1
  placing agency, V9.7
  protected children, V9.3
  security through, CP.23
  sibling placements, CP.30
  step-parent and spouse, V9.3
  in terminal stages of AIDS related illness of
    parent, V9.17
  in UK and settling abroad, V9.20–1
Adoption Act (1976), V1.18, V7.36, V8.3
  Amendments, V9.30
  intercountry adoption, V8.40
  repeals, V9.1
  Section 51, V9.73–5
adoption agency, V9.6
  complaints procedures, V9.15
  procedure for determining payment of
    allowance, V9.7
  records, V7.17
adoption allowance, V9.4–18
  access to records, V9.17–18
  adoption with siblings, V9.9
  amount needed, V9.13
  assessing amount, V9.12–14
  change of circumstances, V9.11
  children with disabilities, V9.9
  circumstances of adopters, V9.15
  commencement date, V9.11–12
  complaints procedures, V9.15
  confidentiality, V9.17–18
  for established relationships, V9.8
  financial needs and resources of child,
    V9.13–14
  financial resources of adopters, V9.12–13
  importance, V9.6
  information for adopters, V9.10–11
  notification to adopters, V9.15–16
  payment by agencies, V9.5
  payment circumstances, V9.7
  payment in principle, V9.9–10
  preservation of records, V9.17–18
  procedure for determining payment, V9.7
  procedures for determining whether should
    be paid, V9.14–15
  review, V9.16–17
  revoked schemes, V9.5
  specific circumstances, V9.8–10
  suspension, V9.17
  termination, V9.16–17
  under revoked scheme, V9.10

variation, V9.16–17
Adoption Allowance (Amendment) Regulations (1991), V9.28–9
Adoption Allowance Regulations (1991), V9.22–7
  amount, V9.24
  circumstances under which paid, V9.23–4
  information, V9.25–6
  procedure in determining whether should be paid, V9.24–5
  records, V9.26
  review, variation and termination, V9.26
Adoption Contact Register, V9.3, V9.19
  advice and counselling, V9.41
  contact address, V9.39
  Information for Adopted People and Their Relatives, V9.31–42
  information on, V9.71
  link, V9.40
  organisations, V9.41–2
  use, V9.35–8
adoption counselling service, V9.19, V9.20, V9.21
  provisions, V9.2, V9.3–4
adoption proceedings, V1.18–19
  GALROs in, V7.15
  section 8 orders, V1.18
Adoption (Scotland) Act (1978), V8.3
adoptive home, visits by adoption agency, V9.17
adoptive parents, social workers' partnership, CP.49–50, CP.51
Adult Psychiatric Service, WT.20
adult-child interaction, V2.38
advance disclosure, V1.3
adventure playgrounds, V2.79
advice
  in after-care, V3.88, V3.89
  after-care responsibility of local authority, V4.98
advisory groups, V2.77
advocacy
  independent visitors' role, V3.78–9
  requirement by child, V4.95–6
  voluntary sector aftercare services, V3.102
  voluntary services, V4.112
  for young people leaving care, V4.108
after-care, V2.12–13, V3.87–8
  advice, V4.97–8
  assistance, V4.7–8
  Careers Service role, V4.116
  complaints, V3.89–90
  from private fostering, V8.24–5
  guide to services, V4.103
  housing department role, V4.113–14
  independent visitors, V3.99
  inter-agency liaison, V4.98
  legal framework, V3.88, V4.98
  local authority powers and duties, V3.88–9
  monitoring schemes, V3.99–100, V4.109
  moving areas, V3.100
  outreach services, CP.12
  parents views in policy, V4.102
  planning provision, V4.101
  powers and duties of local authority, V4.98–100
  preparation for leaving care, V4.101
  probation service involvement, V4.112
  programmes, V3.99
  registered children's homes duties, V3.90–1
  returning to education, V4.116
  school role, V4.115
  social security, V4.116–17
  support, V4.97

support network of friends, V4.106
training and, V4.115–16
transitional arrangements, V3.90, V4.100, V7.38
voluntary sector services, V3.90, V3.102, V4.100, V4.112
young people with disabilities, V3.93–5, V4.103–5
young people's views in policy, V4.102
youth service role, V4.114–15
see also care leavers; preparation for leaving care
age
  care leavers, CP.12
  children in residential care, CP.55
  minimum for secure accomodation, V4.122
  and placement breakdown, CP.68
agencies in child protection, WT.15
  guardians ad litem, WT.16
  health services, WT.17–20
  police, WT.16–17
  reporting officers, WT.16
  social services, WT.15–16
agency case review, WT.125
agency responsibilities, principles, PP.12–15, PP.19–20
  co-operation, PP.15
  dispute procedures, PP.14
  involvement in decisions, PP.13–14
  registers and records, PP.14–15
  review of establishments for placement, PP.15
  support of placements, PP.14
  vulnerable children, PP.14, PP.15
aggression from peers in care, CP.32–3, CP.71
agreements *see* written agreements
AIDS, V3.97
  awareness, V4.107
  education, V4.20
  staff training, V4.20–1
  terminal stages of illness, V9.17
amendments to Act, V7.91–5
American National Day Care Staffing Study, V2.39
appeals, V1.3, V3.113, V4.79
  against court decisions for children living abroad, V8.39–40
  against restriction of liberty, V4.127
  emergency protection orders, V1.60
Appropriate Officer for Disabled Persons (Services, Consultation and Representation) Act, V3.93
area authority, V3.19
Area Child Protection Committee (ACPC), WT.2, WT.117, V1.62, V3.111, V5.6
  abuse in children's homes, V4.32, V4.33, V4.35
  accountability, WT.5
  annual report, WT.115
  case review, WT.125
  Chair, WT.6
  composition, WT.109
  disabled children at risk, V6.45
  finance, WT.7
  handbooks, WT.8
  joint forum, WT.5
  joint policies, WT.5
  organised abuse cases, WT.38–9
  procedures, WT.28, WT.29
  reports, WT.8
  responsibilities, WT.6
  secretariat, WT.6
  senior officer appointments, WT.6
  social services department involvement,

  WT.15–16
  subcommittees, WT.7
  tasks, WT.6–7
  working with agencies, WT.2
  working groups, WT.7
armed services and child protection, WT.22–3, WT.104–6
Army, child protection, WT.104
Arrangements for Placement of Children (General) Regulations (1991), V3.122–30, V4.154–62, V7.39–40
  educational, V4.160
  foster placements, V3.33
  health considerations, V4.160
  records, V3.42
  schedules, V4.159–61
  voluntary organisations, V3.43
Arrangements for Placement of Children Regulations, V3.3–4, V3.5
  welfare of child, V3.6–11
arrest of juveniles by responsible person, V1.77
Asian children, CP.15
assessment, WT.117–18
  of children with disabilities, V6.2, V6.16
  children with special educational needs, V6.23
  comprehensive, WT.31–2
  practice guide for children with disabilities, V6.12
  procedures for children in need, V6.9
  special educational needs, V6.21, V6.28
  for statement of special educational needs, V6.25
  statutory for children with disabilities, V6.21
assistance
  in after-care, V3.88, V3.89
  after-care responsibility of local authority, V4.99
  repayment of financial, V3.89, V4.99
  young people who have been looked after, CP.5
au pairs, V2.79
authorised person, WT.118, V1.21
  applications when juvenile subject to order, V1.75
  care and supervision order applications, V1.23
  emergency protection orders, V1.53
  in recovery orders, V1.65

B

babies, daycare, V2.56
babysitters, V1.7
bail, V1.76
  support schemes, V1.76
Bail Act (1976), V7.46
bedrooms at independent boarding schools, V5.8
befriending
  adult volunteers, V3.96, V4.106
  in after-care, V3.88, V3.89
  after-care responsibility of local authority, V4.98
  by independent visitors, V3.78, V4.94
  children with disabilities, V6.19
  schemes, V2.4
  services, V2.17
  young people who have been looked after, CP.5
behaviour
  at independent boarding schools, V5.11–12

privately fostered child, V8.7

behaviour problems
  analysis, CP.124–9
  of children entering care, CP.7
  with foster children, CP.49
  in residential care, CP.70
benefits see child benefit; social security
  benefits
birth certificate, V9.78
birth family
  importance, CP.22
  preservation, CP.5
birth records, access to, CP.22, V9.19,
  V9.20–1
  Adoption Contact Register, V9.50, V9.61
  counselling, V9.46–8, V9.55, V9.57–8,
    V9.63–71
  Counselling Organisations Outside the
    United Kingdom, V9.79–86
  forms of application, V9.76–7
  from outside UK, V9.79–86
  Information for Adopted People Living
    Outside the UK, V9.51–61
  Information for Adopted People in the UK,
    V9.43–50
  Notes for Counsellors, 0V9.63–71
birth records of adopted children, V9.2
  disclosure, V9.3–4
black children
  in care, CP.16–17
  skin and hair care, V4.27
  see also ethnic minorities; racial origin
Bliss symbols, V8.11
boarded-out children, transitional
  arrangements, V7.39
boarding schools
  gating, V4.18
  health care and education, V4.20
  medication use, V4.21
  personal tutors, V4.11–12
  pupil self-assessment, V4.29
  statement of purpose and function, V4.5
  see also independent boarding schools
Boarding-out of Children (Foster Placement)
  Regulations, V3.28
Boarding-Out Regulations (1988), PP.3, PP.4
books, V4.23
British Sign Language, V6.36
buildings
  access for people with disabilities, V6.38,
    V6.43
  safety for children with disabilities, V6.38
bulk buying, V4.27
bullying, CP.70–1
  children in care, CP.32
Business and Technician Education Council
  (BTEC), V2.33

C

care, V7.36–8
  abduction of children from, WT.82–4, V1.64
  access disputes, CP.26
  admission to, CP.60
  after leaving, V3.99–100
  aggression from peers, CP.32–3
  Asian children, CP.15
  assessment of special educational needs,
    V6.24–5
  assumptions used in decision making,
    CP.71–2, CP.76
  avoidance of disadvantage, PP.11–12

birth family importance, CP.22
  centres, V7.105–13
  children living abroad, V8.37–8, V8.38–9
  compulsory admission, CP.16
  contact with children, WT.67–8, V3.62–3,
    V4.65–6
  continuity of relationships, PP.9–10
  and control orders, V7.36
  crisis admission, CP.18
  cultural issues, CP.35
  deficits in, CP.9–10
  disadvantage of children, CP.7–8
  educational expectations, CP.9
  educational standards, CP.8, CP.9
  effect of changes on child, PP.10
  ethnic minority needs, CP.34–5
  ethnic minority representation, CP.14–15
  extended family, PP.9
  family contact during, PP.9, CP.36
  feelings of shame, V3.97
  identification of learning difficulties, V6.24
  informed choice, PP.8–9
  lack of individual involvement, CP.8
  leaving curve, CP.20, CP.35
  length of stay, CP.16, CP.20
  links with parents, PP.9, CP.24, CP.25–6
  local authority policies on leaving, V4.102–3
  long-term welfare of child, PP.12
  managers, V6.10–11
  medium-term, CP.19
  mixed race parentage, CP.15
  multiple admissions, CP.15
  need for knowledge of origins, CP.22
  parental involvement, PP.9
  personal needs, V6.37, V6.38
  phased, V4.41
  philosophy in children's homes, V4.15
  placement changes, CP.35
  placement with relatives, CP.26–7
  placements, PP.3
  preparation for independence, PP.11
  preparation for leaving, V4.97–8, V4.101,
    V4.105
  principles, PP.4–6
  re-admission rate, CP.15, CP.21
  reasonable, V1.25
  recovery order, V7.31
  relatives in placement provision, CP.36
  remedial service requirements, CP.34
  research programme, CP.1, CP.2
  respite, CP.35–6
  restrictions of contact with children, V4.70–1
  return home, PP.9
  self confidence of child, PP.10–11
  sense of personal identity in child, PP.10
  shared arrangements, V1.9–10
  short term, V4.4
  sibling group admissions, CP.27–8
  siblings, PP.9
  stigmatisation risk, PP.11–12
  stress from peers, CP.32
  time span, PP.10
  transition arrangements for emigration,
    V7.41
  transitional arrangements, V7.36–8
  wardship proceedings, V7.36
  white orientation of system, CP.17
  without parental responsibility, V6.4
  written agreements, CP.43
  see also respite care
care, after leaving, V4.108–10
  moving away, V4.109
  notifying local authority, V4.110
  social services responsibilities, V4.109

Care of Children: Principles and Practice in
  Regulations and Guidance, V8.1
care, entry to
  behavioural problems, CP.7
  development problems, CP.7
  educational deficits, CP.7
  health of child, CP.7
  social conditions, CP.6–7
care leavers, CP.9–13
  accomodation, CP.11–12, CP.34
  advice, CP.13
  age, CP.12
  assistance, CP.13
  classification of needs, CP.59
  day to day problems, CP.34
  employment training, CP.11
  ethnic group, CP.13–17
  financial help, CP.61
  loneliness, CP.34
  outreach services, CP.12–13
  personal balance sheet, CP.90–1
  pregnancy incidence, CP.11
  relationships for, CP.12
  resources for, CP.12
  schemes for, CP.10
  support for, CP.10
  well-being, CP.12
  see also after-care; preparation for leaving
    care
care, long-term
  admission on court orders, CP.20
  breakdown, CP.19–20
  effects of, CP.35
  ethnic origins of children, CP.16
  identification of children, CP.20
  outcome, CP.19
  placement change, CP.18
  premature endings, CP.18
  returning home problems, CP.19–20
  risk of instability, CP.18–20
care management, V6.10
  and child care practice, V6.10
  needs-led, V6.10
  practice guide, 12
care order, V1.20–1
  abolition in criminal proceedings, V1.72
  access and contact, V7.37
  age of child, V1.23
  appeals against, V1.34–5
  applications for, V1.21–7
  conditions for, V1.23–6
  considerations in applications, V1.21–3
  contact with children, V1.36–9
  and contact orders, V1.11
  court requirements, V1.26–7
  criteria for, WT.26
  discharge, V1.18, V1.20, V1.33–4, V1.36
  effect, V1.35–6
  harm to child, V1.23–4
  legal framework, WT.66
  Northern Ireland, V7.30
  order making powers, V1.21
  and parental responsibility, V2.73–4, V2.75,
    V6.3, V6.4
  party status, V1.26–7
  pending appeal, V1.35
  placement with parents, V3.45–7
  with relative or friend, V3.28
  repeat applications, V1.34
  review, V1.33–4
  section 8 order discharge, V1.18, V1.36
  shared, V1.11
  threshold criteria, V1.24
  timetable, V1.27

transfer, V7.30–1, V7.79–80
transitional arrangements, V1.79–80
variation, V1.20
and wardship, V1.42
care order, interim, WT.68, WT.122–3, V1.27, V1.28–33
child's consent to examination or assessment, V1.31–2
criteria, V1.28
duration, V1.28, V1.29–30
effects, V1.32–3
medical and psychiatric assessment, V1.28, V1.29, V1.30–2
responsibilities arising from, V1.32–3
care plan
continuing, V4.101
preparation for leaving care, V3.95, V4.105
care proceedings, WT.66–7
transitional arrangements, V1.71, V1.72
welfare principle application, V1.2
care, short-term
accomodation provision, CP.21
achievements, CP.18–19
care, temporary, ethnic origins of children, CP.16
careers guidance, V3.105–6, V4.115
Careers Service
advice for people with disabilities, V6.49
preparation for leaving care, V3.106
role in after-care, V4.116
caregivers
confidentiality of information, PP.13
resources for, PP.14
training, V2.33
carers
in child's home, V2.79
health, V3.52
involvement in careers guidance, V4.115
own children's problems, CP.50, CP.51
partnership with parents, CP.39–41
in review of children's cases, V3.83–4, V4.60, V4.61–2
suitability, V3.51
support, 356–7
training, PP.14
visits, V3.58–9
Caring for People, V6.9
case records, V4.28–9
access to, V4.29
retention, V4.29
case reviews, WT.57–60
public concern, WT.57, WT.59
catering arrangements for children's homes, V4.25–7
cautioning, V1.71
Central Council for Education and Training in Social Work, WT.54, V7.24
Channel Islands, care orders, V7.31
Charge and Control Regulations, PP.3
charging for services, V2.13–14
child
abuse *see* abuse
attending review meetings, V4.61
in consultation about review of children's cases, V4.60
consultation in decision making, V2.11–12
contribution to decisions, PP.11
informed choice of care, V8.-9
preparation for independence, V1.1
views in placement with parents, V3.53–4
child assessment order, WT.29, WT.119, V1.45–51, V4.123
application, WT.95–103, V1.45
for children with disabilities, V6.45

commencement, V1.46–7
conditions, V1.45–6
contacts during, V1.48, V3.64, V4.67
directions of court, V1.47
duration, V1.46–7, V1.51
with education supervision orders, V1.49
effects, V1.47
failure to produce child, V1.49
further assessment, V1.50
keeping child away from home, V1.47–8
multi-disciplinary assessment, V1.50–1
parental co-operation, V1.50–1
Part V of Act, WT.73–4
practice issues, V1.50–1
prior investigations, V1.46
procedural requirements, V1.48
with section 8 orders, V1.49
child benefit
in adoption, V9.8
for foster parents, V8.8
see also benefits
Child Care Act (1980), V2.1
access order, V7.37
boarded-out children, V7.39
criminal care orders, V7.44
emigration of children in care, V7.41
transitional arrangements, V1.79
welfare of child, V4.38
child development
in day care services, V2.37
and district handicap teams, V6.28
Child Minding and Day Care (Applications for Registration)
Regulations (1991), V8.51–4
amendment, V8.57–8
Child Minding and Day Care (Registration and Inspection Fees)
Regulations, V8.55–6
amendment, V8.57–8
child protection *see* protection of children
child protection conference, WT.31, WT.41–7, CP.71–2, WT.118
administrative arrangements, WT.47
agencies involved, WT.45–6
agreement between professionals, family and child, WT.42
attendance, WT.45–6
chairing, WT.46
children's involvement in decisions, WT.43
conflict of interests, WT.43, WT.44
decisions not to register, WT.45
exclusion from, WT.43–4
friend's and supporter's presence, WT.44
initial, WT.41–2
involvement of children, parents and carers, WT.43
key worker, WT.42, WT.43
minutes, WT.44
organisation, WT.42–3
participation of children and family adults, WT.45
pre-birth, WT.49
preparation for, WT.47
purpose, WT.41–2
records of, WT.47
reports, WT.47
responsibility to convene, WT.41
Child Protection Coordinator, V4.33
child protection plan, WT.18
abuser going to prison, WT.32
child involvement, WT.32
child protection register, WT.107
comprehensive assessment, WT.32
de-registration, WT.33

implementation, WT.32, WT.33
need for, WT.48
parental involvement, WT.32
review, WT.33
child protection register, WT.47–51, WT.119
abuse management information, WT.113
case record confidentiality, WT.51
categories of abuse, WT.48–9
child protection plan, WT.107
computerised records, WT.50
criteria for registration, WT.48
custodian, WT.50
data held on, WT.107
de-registration criteria, WT.49–50
identification of people involved, WT.107
key worker, WT.107
management, WT.50
nature of abuse, WT.107
notification to school, WT.21–2
purpose, WT.48
relevant offences by members and visitors to household, WT.51
removal of child's name, WT.33
removal of names, WT.44–5, WT.50
requirements for registration, WT.48
child protection review, WT.42, WT.125
de-registration consideration, WT.49
child protection work
agencies involved in, WT.15–24
records, WT.13
specialist advice, WT.15
Childline, WT.23
childminders, V2.79
in child protection, WT.22
for children with disabilities, V6.19–20
fees for registration and inspection, V8.36
fire safety guidance, V2.82
first aid training, V2.35
inspection, V2.63–4
premises, V2.63
re-registration, V8.36
records, V2.63
referees, V8.35
register, V2.58–9
registration, V2.49–62, V6.19–20, V8.31, V8.34
relationship with parents, V2.46
respite care by, V6.33
transitional arrangements, V7.43
welfare of children, V2.63
childminding, V2.16–17, V2.45–6
contracts, V2.46
and day care services, V2.28
equipment, V2.46
health checks, V8.35
LEA advice, V6.24
overnight stays, V8.31
police checks, V8.35–6
premises, V2.45
and private fostering, V8.30–1
records, V2.46
respite care, V8.31
services, V2.2
staff/child ratios, V2.45
toys, V2.46
Children Act 1989 (Commencement No. 2) Order (1991), V7.88–90
Children Act 1989 (Commencement and Transitional Provisions) Order (1991), V7.85–7
Children Act 1989 (Consequential Amendment of Enactments) Order (1991), V7.132–3
Children Act (1975), custodianship orders, V7.36

Children Act Regulation Amendments, V7.137
Children (Allocation of Proceedings) Order
(1991), V7.14, V7.98–113
  allocation to county courts, V7.116–17
  care centres, V7.105–13
  commencement of proceedings, V7.114–16
  family court committee structure, V7.118–19
  family hearing centres, V7.104
children living abroad
  appeals against court decisions, V8.39–40
  consideration of, V8.38–9
  looked after by local authority, V8.37–40
children looked after by local authority see
  looked after children
Children (Prescribed Orders) Regulations
(1991), V7.78–82
Children (Private Arrangements for Fostering)
  Regulations (1991), V8.42–5
Children (Representations, Placements and
  Reviews) Regulations
(1991), V7.134–6
Children (Secure Accomodation) (No. 2)
  Regulations (1991), V7.83–4
Children (Secure Accomodation) Regulations
(1991), V4.180–5
Children and Young Person's Act (1933)
children sentenced under, V4.123
detention, V4.129
Children and Young Persons Act (1963), place
  of safety orders, V7.42
Children and Young Persons Act (1966)(Act of
  Tynwald), V7.30–1
Children and Young Persons Act (1969),
  V1.21, V1.23, V1.42
  amendments, V7.80–1
  criminal care orders, V7.44
  criminal proceedings, V1.73
  criminal supervision orders, V7.42
  interim care orders, V7.36
  interpretation by local authorities, CP.60
  maximum period of restriction of liberty,
    V4.126–7
  place of safety orders, V7.42
  private fostering, V8.3
  remanded children, V4.123–4
  supervision order on educational grounds,
    V7.22
  supervision orders, V7.42
  transfer of care orders, V7.30
  transitional arrangements, V1.79, V1.80,
    V7.40, V7.41
children's homes, V4.1–5
  after-care duties of registered, V4.100–1
  aims and objectives, V4.5–7
  behaviour standards, V4.16
  behavioural methods, V4.11
  child abuse in, V4.32–5
  children with disabilities, V4.4
  control, V4.15
  decor, V4.14
  definitions, V4.2–3
  diet in, V4.25
  facilities, V4.6
  and fostering, V3.34–5
  framework of practice, V4.2
  good practice, V4.2, V4.4
  health records, V4.20–1
  health and safety, V4.35
  homework facilities, V4.22–3
  hygiene in food preparation, V4.27
  independent boarding schools as, V5.2
  inspection, V4.4–5
  involvement of children in decisions, V4.16
  medication use, V4.21

neighbourhood relationships, V4.13
notification of children accomodated in
  certain establishments, V4.36–7
notification of serious occurrences, WT.36
office space, V4.13
physical restraint, V4.15–16
placements, V4.1
practical and financial skill learning, V4.108
privacy, V4.14
psychotherapeutic methods, V4.11
purpose, V4.1
registration, V4.31–2
registration checks, V4.35
relationships between staff and children,
  V4.16
requirements, V4.1–2
review of children accomodated by, V4.38
schools, V4.3–4
services, V4.6
short term care, V4.4
staff group composition, V4.9
support for staff, V4.9
telephone facilities, V4.12, V4.13
transitional arrangements by private, V7.42
upkeep, V4.14
visitors, V4.8, V4.13
welfare of children, V4.2, V4.12
children's homes regulations
  absence of person in charge, V4.30–1
  absence without authority, V4.30
  accomodation, V4.12
  availability of, V4.30
  case records, V4.28–9
  catering arrangements, V4.25–7
  clothing provision, V4.27–8
  community homes, V4.31
  competence of staff, V4.7
  decoration and furnishing, V4.14
  disabled children, V4.15
  disciplinary measures, V4.16–19
  education, V4.21–3
  employment, V4.23–4
  establishment numbers, V4.7
  external consultancy, V4.11
  fire precautions, V4.28
  good order and discipline, V4.15–16
  health, V4.19–21
  laundry, V4.15–16
  local authority visits, V4.32
  location planning, V4.12–13
  notification of significant events, V4.30
  organisation of care, V4.11–12
  personal requisites, V4.27–8
  records on homes, V4.30
  religion, V4.24–5
  responsible authority accountability and
    visiting, V4.31
  staff meetings, V4.11
  staff supervision, V4.10–11
  staffing, V4.7
  statement of purpose and function, V4.5–7
  structure and layout, V4.13–14
  training, V4.23–4
  vetting staff, V4.8–9
  voluntary home registration, V4.31
  written guidance for staff, V4.9–10
Children's Homes Regulations (1991),
  V4.133–53
  administration, V4.140–2
  applications for registration as registered
    home, V4.150–1
  applications for registration of voluntary
    homes, V4.149–50
  change of person in charge, V4.152

community homes, V4.142
conduct of children's homes, V4.136–40
confidential records, V4.147–8
introduction, V4.135–6
local authority visits, V4.144–5
notification of particulars of voluntary homes,
  V4.144
particulars relating to voluntary homes,
  V4.152
records, V4.148–9
registered children's homes, V4.143–4
registration of voluntary homes, V4.143
revocations, V4.145
schedules, V4.145–52
statement to be kept, V4.145–6
Chronically Sick and Disabled Persons Act
(1970), V2.9, V2.13, V3.14, V3.94, V6.9,
V6.55
  in placement of children arrangements,
    V4.50
Chronically Sick and Disabled Persons Act
(1986), V4.104
circumcision
  female, V8.19–20
  male, V8.20
Citizens' Advice Bureau, V3.102
  advice on social security benefits, V4.117
Civil Legal Aid (General) (Amendment) (No. 2)
  Regulations (1991), V7.123–7
Clerk to the Justices, on GALRO Panel
  Committee, V7.7
clothing
  allowances, V4.28
  distinctive or inappropriate, V4.18
  provision, V4.27–8
codes of practice, PP.2
coeliac disease, V4.20
cohabitees, suitability as careers, V3.51, V3.52
Commissioner for Local Administration, V3.113
committee structure, V2.77
common rooms at independent boarding
  schools, V5.8–9
communication
  with children with disabilities, V6.14–15
  comprehensibility, PP.13
  contact decisions, V4.71–2
  difficulties in child protection interviews,
    WT.30
  in health care of children, V4.20
  independent visitor with child with
    disabilities, V6.32
  support, V3.95
  support for young people with disabilities,
    V4.104
communication skills
  children's home staff, V4.8
  fostered children, V8.11
community
  health services, WT.19
  mental handicap teams, V6.28
  responsibilities in child protection, WT.24
  service order, V7.46
  support for disabled people, V6.49
community care, V6.9–10
  local authorities, V2.3–4
  primary health care team, V6.50–1
  published information, V6.11
  SSD assessment of people, V6.10
community homes, V4.142
  restriction of liberty, V4.120
  secure accomodation notification, V4.124
complaints, V3.108, V3.109
  advice to staff, V3.111
  after-care preparation, V4.99

against independent boarding schools,
V5.15
avenues of, V3.113–14
on child's behalf, V4.76
consideration by panel, V4.84–5
eligibility, V3.118, V4.84
failure of responsible authority, V3.114
oral, V3.117–18, V4.83
panel, V3.117, V3.119
receipt, V3.117
records of, V4.86
reference to panel, V3.118–20
subjects of, V4.76
and unresolved problems, V4.77
complaints procedures, WT.119, V4.77
at independent boarding schools, V5.13
availability of information, V6.42–3
children with disabilities, V6.41–3
monitoring, V3.120–1
setting up, V3.116–20, V4.82–6
staff for, V4.81
support from outside, V6.42
transitional arrangements for children in
care, V7.37
comprehensive assessment, WT.118
compulsory orders, PP.8
compulsory powers, CP.39–40
confidentiality of information, WT.11–12
medical, WT.12
nursing, WT.12
and protection of child, WT.12–13
conflict, children as victims of, CP.44
consultation, transitional arrangements for
children in care, V7.37
contact, V4.65
arrangements, V4.68
and child protection orders, V4.67–8
with children in care, V4.65–6
with children in residential care, V4.69
child's wishes, V4.69–70
costs of visits, V4.69
decisions, V4.71–2
disagreements over, V4.72
importance, V4.66–7
leaflets about, V4.72
legislative framework, V4.65
and placement, V4.68
plans for, V4.68
records of, V4.73
refusal, V4.70
restrictions with children in care, V4.70–1
reviewing, V4.72–3
setting for visits, V4.68–9
suspension, V4.71
transitional arrangements for children in
care, V7.37
travel arrangements, V4.69
variation, V4.71
contact with children being looked after, V3.62
and child protection orders, V3.64–5
child's wishes, V3.67
communication of decisions, V3.69
court decisions, V3.68
delay in decisions, V3.68
departure from terms of court order, V3.68
disagreement with parents, V3.69–70
expenses, V3.66–7
importance, V3.63–4
legal advice, V3.68
placement, V3.65
planning, V3.65
residential care, V3.66
restrictions, V3.67–8
reviews, V3.70

sanctions, V3.66
support, V3.65
suspension, V3.69
travel arrangements, V3.66–7
variation, V3.69
visits, V3.65–6
Contact with Children Regulations, V3.62,
V3.63
Contact with Children Regulations (1991),
V1.38, V3.150–1, V4.169–70
contact order, WT.67–8, WT.119, V1.9, V1.11
application, V1.13
legal framework, WT.70
contacts, review of children's cases, V3.85
continuity, child's need for, PP.4
contraception, V3.97, V4.107
contributions towards cost of maintenance,
V2.14
control of child, V3.66
corporal punishment, V4.17
at independent boarding schools, V5.12
councillors, complaints to, V3.113, V4.79
counselling
for children in need, V6.5
in education supervision orders, V7.25–6
self-acceptance, V3.97–8
voluntary sector aftercare services, V3.102
voluntary services, V4.112
young people with disabilities, V3.98
counsellors, guidance for access to birth
records, V9.63–71
county courts, V1.2
family proceedings, V1.21
County Courts Act (1984), V1.34
court
action in individual cases, WT.25–6
adjournment, V4.127
care orders, WT.66–7
child assessment orders, WT.69–70
consideration of orders, V1.17–18
decision making, WT.1
delay, V1.17
duties, PP.5
duty when considering making orders,
V1.16–17
education supervision orders, V7.23–4
emergency procedures, WT.68–9, WT.70
family assistance orders, WT.70
guardian ad litem appointment, WT.71
initial hearing, WT.25
interim orders, WT.68
knowledge of procedure, WT.2
making of orders, WT.63
new orders, WT.70
non-adversarial stance, V1.3
parents at disadvantage, CP.45
power to deal with restriction of liberty,
V7.33–4
powers in applications for secure
accomodation, V4.126–7
preparation of child for hearing, V4.125
private law orders, WT.1
reports on education supervision orders,
V7.24–5
sentencing powers under Criminal Justice
Act (1991), V7.46–7
statutory checklist, V1.17
transfer of cases between, 3, V1.2
welfare of child, WT.1, WT.63
welfare officer, WT.119
welfare principle in making orders, V.12,
V1.17
youth, V7.47
see also section 8 orders

court order, V1.1, V2.75
appeals against, V4.79
for children with disabilities, V6.44–7
contact, V3.68
contact arrangements, V4.65, V4.66, V4.67,
V4.68
criteria for, WT.26
departure from terms of contact order, V3.68
departures from under section 34, V4.71
for parental responsibility, V6.3, V6.4
placement of children, V3.5
private, V1.2
regarding contact, V3.62–3
welfare principle application, V1.2
court proceedings
delay, V1.1–2
independent visitor in, V4.95
prevention of delay, V7.2–3
Courts and Legal Services Act (1990), V4.99
amendments to Act in, V7.91–5
transitional arrangements, V1.79
creches, V2.40, V2.78
Credit Accumulation and Transfer System,
WT.54
crime prevention, V1.69–71
criminal care order, V1.72
transitional arrangements, V7.44
criminal implications of act, V1.1
criminal injuries compensation, V1.7
Criminal Justice Act (1988)
and child protection work, WT.10
remanded children, V4.124
Criminal Justice Act (1991), WT.30, V7.34,
V7.45–7
arrest and detention of juveniles, V7.45–6
children's evidence, V7.45
juvenile remands, V7.46
parental responsibility, V7.46
sentencing powers of court, V7.46–7
Criminal Justice Bill, V1.78
criminal proceedings, WT.16, WT.17
abolition of care orders, V1.72
evidence for, WT.13
criminal records
of prospective boarding school staff, V5.7–8
of staff, V4.8–9
criminal supervision orders, V1.72–5
and education supervision orders, V7.28
residence requirements, V1.4, V1.73–5
transitional arrangements, V7.42
Crown Prosecution Service
criminal proceedings, WT.16, WT.17
in organised abuse cases, WT.39
cultural background, V4.24
clothing, V4.27
in placement of children arrangements,
V4.43, V4.46–7
questionnaire, CP.106–9
cultural ethos in independent boarding schools,
V5.11
cultural issues in care, CP.35
cultural minorities
youth service needs, V3.105
youth service role, V4.115
culture
and placement of children in care with
parents, V3.51
in welfare of child, CP.5
curfew orders, V7.47–8
custodians, allowances, V7.36
custody orders, V7.36
cystic fibrosis, foster parents' knowledge of
care, V6.36

D

data, obtaining, CP.89
Data Protection Act (1984), child protection work, WT.11
DATA syndrome, CP.46, CP.51
day care facilities
  consultation for review, V2.67
  data for review, V2.67
  inspection, V2.63–4
  premises, V2.63
  records, V2.63
  report of review, V2.67–8
  review, V2.65–8
  terms of reference for review, V2.66
  welfare of children, V2.63
day care providers
  fire safety training, V2.81
  health and safety requirements, V2.83–4
day care services, WI.120, V2.1, V2.2, V2.4, V2.15–18, V2.24–5
  activities, V2.32
  adult-child interaction, V2.38
  applications for registration, V8.34–5
  befriending services, V2.17
  behaviour, V2.36
  in child protection, WT.22
  and childminding, V2.16–17, V2.28
  for children with disabilities, V2.34, V6.19–20
  for children in need, V6.5
  for children not in need, V2.26
  co-operation in provision, V2.26–7
  co-ordination function, V2.25
  combined with nursery education, V2.44
  day nurseries, V2.16
  development, V2.27–8
  drop-in centres, V2.18
  education in, V2.40
  equal opportunities, V2.34
  exemptions from registration, V2.53
  extended day playgroups, V2.40, V2.78
  fit person, V2.54
  food, V2.42, V2.43
  food hygiene, V2.35–6
  full day care, V2.40–2
  full day for school age children, V2.47–8
  furniture and equipment, V2.42, V2.48
  good practice, V2.32
  group sizes, V2.42, V2.47
  happiness of children, V2.40
  health issues, V2.35–6
  health and safety conditions, V2.39
  holiday schemes, V2.17
  independently run, V2.16, V2.27
  information, V2.30–1
  interpersonal relationships, V2.39
  advisory and support services, V6.24
  learning opportunities, V2.39
  managements, V2.35
  observation, V2.42, V2.43
  occasional, V2.54
  open access facilities, V2.48
  out-of-school clubs, V2.17
  outings, V2.47
  oversight, V2.25
  parent/toddler groups, V2.17–18
  parental involvement, V2.34–5
  parents' need, V2.30
  peer interactions, V2.38–9
  playbuses, V2.18
  playgroups, V2.16
  police checks, V8.35–6
  policy development, V2.25
  premises, V2.41–2, V2.47

public liability insurance, V2.36
quality of care, V2.36–40, V2.40
racial groups, V2.34
records, V2.42, V2.43, V2.48
referees, V8.35
register, V2.58–9
regulations, V8.51–8
report on provision, V2.24
responsibilities, V2.25
review, V2.26
review duties of SSDs, V6.20
sanctions, V2.36
for school age children, V2.46–8
sessional, V2.43, V2.47–8
space standards, V2.41–2, V2.43
stability of care, V2.39
staff/child ratios, V2.41, V2.43
staffing, V2.36
standards, V2.32–3, V2.40–5
supervised activities, V2.17
toy libraries, V2.18
toys, V2.42
training of caregivers, V2.24, V2.33
unit sizes, V2.42
voluntary organisations, V2.27
see also registration system for day care facilities
day nurseries, V2.16, V2.40, V2.78
  places for children with disabilities, V6.13
death of child, WT.57, V4.30, V8.15
debt, CP.11
decisions, chairing meetings, CP.134–5
Definition of Independent Visitors (Children) Regulations (1991), V3.152–3, V4.178–9
dental treatment, and placement of children arrangements, V4.43
Department of Health Consultancy Service, V4.30, V7.12
  independent boarding school staff checks, V5.7
Department of Health Consultancy Services Register, V4.8, V4.93
Department of Health Guidance and Reports, V6.60
Department of Social Security, income-support role, V3.101
deprivation, CP.6
  effects of care, CP.7
  problems associated with, CP.7
DES list 99, V4.8–9, V5.7
detained children, V4.123–4
detention under Children and Young Person's Act (1933), V4.129
development
  impairment, V1.24–5
  minor shortcomings, V1.25
  in private fostering, V8.6
  quality of substitute care, V2.30
developmental assessment, WT.118
diabetes, V4.20
diet
  in children's homes, V4.25
  special, V4.20
directions
  appointment, WT.25
  transitional arrangements, V7.38
disabilities, assessment of children with, V6.2
  continuing reassessment, V6.9
  for court orders, V6.44–5
  local authority, V2.10
  procedures, V6.9
disabilities, children with, V2.9
  accomodation in independent boarding schools, V6.40

adoption allowance, V9.9
aids for, V6.18
befriending schemes, V6.19
child assessment order, V6.45
co-ordination of services, V6.7–8
communication difficulties, V6.14–15
complaints procedures, V4.79, V6.41–3
complex needs, V6.14
consent to medical treatment or examination, V6.46
continuing need for services, V6.9, V6.11–12
counselling of family, V6.8, V6.24
day care services, V2.34, V6.19–20
decision-making, V6.14
delivery of services, V6.42
early identification, V6.28
effect on parents, V6.19
emergency protection order, V6.45–6
family centres, V6.18–19
foster placements, V6.35–7
Guardians ad Litem for, V6.46–7
health surveillance, V6.27
home care service, V6.18
housing, V6.18
identification of, V6.7–8
independent visitor for those in residential care, V6.31–2
integration of services, V2.10
integration and special health care needs, V6.28
interviews in protection cases, WT.30
involvement in planning, V6.14
living environment, V6.36–7
living with family, V6.18–20
management process, V6.11–12
minority ethnic groups, V6.65
need for ongoing support, V6.48–9
needs of brothers and sisters, V6.13–14
notification of accomodation to SSD, V6.39–40
parental responsibility, V6.3–4, V6.30
placement in accomodation, V6.30–4
and placement of children arrangements, V4.43
planning for future, V6.29
planning post-school provision, V6.50–2
planning residential placement, V6.32
prevention of secondary handicaps, V6.51
principles of work with, V6.2
privacy, V6.37, V6.38
private fostering, V8.9
protection, V6.44–7
provision of services, V6.1
publication of management and assessment arrangements, V6.11–12
recruitment of foster parents, V6.35–6
register, V6.7–8
registration, V2.9–10
representations procedures, V6.41–3
residential care, V6.38–40
respite care, V6.18, V6.32–3
reunification with family, V6.31
role of child health services, V6.27–9
safeguards for, V6.1
self esteem, PP.11
services for, V6.1–2, V6.53–4, V6.61–2
services for privately fostered children, V8.19
short-term residential care, V6.32–3
social security benefits, V6.58–9
SSD functions, V6.1
standards of service, V6.11
suitability of accomodation, V6.36–7
training and support for foster parents, V6.36

transition to adulthood, V6.48–52
views on plans for welfare, V6.14
vulnerability, V6.46
disabilities, young people with
after-care, V3.99
benefits, V3.107
careers advice, V4.116
children's homes, V4.4, V4.15
communication support, V3.95
community support, V6.52
complaints procedure, V3.113
counselling, V3.98
education, V3.95
further education, V3.105, V4.115
housing, V3.94
independent living, V6.51
leaving care, V3.93–5, V4.103–5
needs, V3.94, V3.105
personal development, V6.52
potential, V3.94
practical skills, V3.98
publications, V6.65–6
relationship development, V4.106
residential care, V6.51
return home from residential care, V6.51
self-esteem development, V4.107
sexual development, V6.52
social security benefits, V4.117
specialist education, V6.52
staff training for children's homes, V4.8
vocational training, V6.52
welfare services, V3.94
wishes and perceptions, V6.52
youth service role, V3.105, V4.114–15
disability
definition, V6.5
provision of services for people with, V6.2
disabled facilities grant, V6.57
disabled people, access to buildings, V6.38
Disabled Persons Act (1986), V6.9, V6.10
involvement in education, V6.25
in placement of children arrangements,
V4.50
working with LEA, V6.49
young people over 16, V6.26
Disabled Persons (Services, Consultation and
Representation) Act (1986), V3.94, V6.55–6
assessment, V3.14
local authorities, V2.9
Disablement Resettlement Officer, V3.106,
V4.116
disciplinary measures in child abuse cases,
V5.7
disciplinary procedure, V4.80
discipline
at independent boarding schools, V5.11–12
in children's homes, V4.15–19
permitted measures, V4.16–17
prohibited measures, V4.17–19
discrimination in children's lives, PP.11
Disqualification for Caring for Children
Regulations, V8.46–50
disqualification from caring for children,
V8.32–3
appeal, V8.33
grounds, V8.32
lifting, V8.32–3
local authority provision, V8.33
district health authorities (DHAs)
accomodation for children with disabilities,
V6.39–40
in child protection, WT.17–18, WT.19
co-operation with SSDs for children with
disabilities, V6.28

information to LEAs on special educational
needs, V6.23
private fostering of children with disabilities,
V8.9
provision of information on voluntary groups,
V6.23
range of services for children with
disabilities, V6.53–4
role for children in need, V6.7
transitional arrangements for children in
care, V7.43
divorce, parental responsibility, V2.74
doctor, designated senior, WT.120
documentary evidence preparation, V1.3
Domestic Proceedings and Magistrates' Courts
Act (1978), V1.19, V1.52
Domestic Violence and Matrimonial
Proceedings Act (1976), V1.52
domicilary services for children in need, V6.5
drop-in centres, V2.18, V3.99
voluntary sector aftercare services, V3.102
voluntary services, V4.112

E

education
children in care, CP.7, CP.8, CP.9, CP.34
children in homes, V4.21–3
designated staff, WT.120–1
determinants of school achievement, CP.9
for disabled young people, V4.115
discontinuity, CP.9
expenses, V3.89
financial assistance from local authority,
V3.101
further for children with disabilities, V6.48
grant, V4.99
health, V4.20
help in obtaining, V4.23
home on trial placements, CP.9
local authority assistance, V3.106–7
otherwise than at school, V7.26
placement of children, V3.9–10
and placement of children arrangements,
V4.43, V4.45–6
and placement of children in care with
parents, V3.50
preparation for leaving care, V3.105–6
of privately fostered child, V8.9
promotion, V4.22
records for child protection work, WT.11
returning to after leaving care, V4.116
review of children's cases, V3.85, V3.86
school non-attendance, V1.63
sexual, V3.97
support from children's home, V4.22
young people with disabilities, V3.95, V6.50,
V6.52
see also local education authority (LEA)
Education Act (1944)
care proceedings, V7.22
education supervision orders, V7.23–4
Education Act (1980), V8.28–9
nursery education, V2.24
Education Act (1981), V3.14, V6.56
assessment of children in need, V6.9
integration of children with special needs,
V6.25
parents in assessment procedures, V6.23
in placement of children arrangements,
V4.50
special educational needs, V6.10

statements of special educational need,
V4.46
Education (Mandatory Awards) Regulations
(1991), V6.57
Education Reform Act (1988), V6.56
education services
in child protection, WT.21–2
for children with disabilities, V6.21–6
for young children, V2.4
Education (Special Educational
Needs)(Approval of Independent Schools)
Regulations (1991), V6.57
education supervision orders, V6.25–6,
V7.22–9
with care orders or supervision orders, V7.26
ceasing, V7.27–8
change of schools, V7.26–7
with child assessment orders, V1.49
child subject to other orders, V7.28
consultation, V7.23
court powers and responsibilities, V7.23–4
directions used by supervising officer, V7.27
extending, V7.27–8
grounds for application, V7.23–9
parents right of appeal, V7.28
preparation for, V7.25
removal of parents' rights, V7.25, V7.26
scope of legislation, V7.22–3
SSD duties, V7.28
supervising officer, V7.24, V7.25–6
welfare of child, V7.22–3, V7.24
Education Welfare Service, V7.25
electronic monitoring, V7.47
emergency procedures, WT.68–9
emergency protection order (EPO), WT.121,
V1.51–60
in adoption proceedings, V9.1–2
appeal, V1.60
application, WT.87–94, V1.52–3
application procedure, V1.55
assessment of child, V1.59
authorised persons, V1.53
child assessment order consequence, V1.49
child in refuge, V1.60, V4.131
for children with disabilities, V6.45–6
contact with child, V3.64, V4.67
contact of child with parents, V1.58, V1.59
court directions, V1.58–9
criteria for, WT.26
discharge, V1.60
disclosure of child's whereabouts, V1.56
duration, V1.59
effects, V1.56
evidence requirement, V1.52
ex parte hearing, V1.55
extension, V1.59
frustrated access, V1.46, V1.53–4
granting ex parte, WT.25
grounds for application, V1.48, V1.53–5
guardians ad litem involvement, WT.16,
V7.16
for immediate protection, WT.27–8
legal framework, WT.68, WT.70
local authority accomodation, V3.2
looked after children, V4.38
medical examination, V1.59
obstruction of search, V1.57
parental responsibility, V6.3
Part V of Act, WT.74–8
powers of entry, V1.56–7
psychiatric examination, V1.59
recovery order, V7.31
removal of alleged abuser, V1.52
removal of child, V1.58

return of child, V1.58
search for child, V1.56
significant harm risk, V1.54–5
subsequent removal, V1.58
warrant for police officer, V1.57
Emergency Protection Order (Transfer of Responsibilities) Regulations (1991), V1.52–3, V7.96–7
emigration, transitional arrangements for children in care, V7.41
emotional abuse, WT.49
employers, health and safety responsibilities, V2.84
employment
  expenses, V4.99
  financial assistance, V3.101, V4.111
  help in obtaining, V4.23
  local authority assistance, V3.101, V3.106–7
  opportunities for children in care, CP.34
  registering for, V4.24
end of year figures, CP.54
environmental health departments in registration of daycare services, V2.51
epilepsy, V4.20
equal opportunities
  day care services, V2.34
  legislation, V3.109
equipment loans, V6.16
ethnic minority groups
  in care, CP.34–5
  care leavers, CP.13–17
  classification, CP.58
  counselling, V3.98
  health care, V3.8, V4.44
  relationship development, V4.106
  self image, PP.11
  self-esteem development, V4.107
  youth service role, V3.105, V4.115
ethnic origin of foster parents, V3.26
evidence
  of children, V7.45
  for criminal proceedings, WT.13
  importance, CP.77–8
  in planning, CP.72, CP.76
  quality of, CP.2
  standard for child protection purposes, WT.39
  testing, CP.134–7
  working tools, CP.89
expenses, after-care, V3.89
expert witnesses, in child assessment order, V6.45
exploitation, entitlement to protection from, PP.7

F

family, V1.1
  aides, V2.23, V6.13
  assessment, WT.118
  breakdown, CP.7
  in care of children with disabilities, V6.13
  child with disabilities living with, V6.18–20
  child of, V1.13
  chronic illness effects, V6.40
  harm from unnecessary intervention, WT.27
  hearing centres, V7.104
  help with relationships, CP.34
  importance in children's lives, V6.4
  intact, CP.6
  involvement in placement of children arrangements, V4.49
  networks, CP.34

normal life, PP.8
partnership with, WT.1–2
  in placement of children, V3.13
preservation, CP.5
relationship development of young person, V4.106
relatives for placement, CP.26–7, CP.36
report preparation for education supervision order, V7.25
respite care, CP.35–6, V6.32–3, V6.33
return to from foster care, V3.40–1
services for with children in need, V6.5
socially disadvantaged, CP.36
stress, CP.7
upbringing of children within, V2.22
family assistance orders, WT.121, V1.15–16, V1.42, V2.75–6
  legal framework, WT.70
  with section 8 orders, V1.16
family centres, WT.121, V2.18–20
  for chidren with disabilities, V6.18–19
  community, V2.19
  parental representation, CP.43
  self-help, V2.19
  therapeutic, V2.19
family contact with child
  in care, CP.36, V4.65, V4.67, V4.68
  with disabilities in accomodation, V6.31
  living apart, V4.66
  and placement of children arrangements, V4.43
  in placement of children in care with parents, V3.50
  and re-unification, V2.13
Family Court Business Committee, V7.15
  specialist advice sources, V7.20
Family Court Committee, WT.23
  structure, V7.118–19
family, extended, PP.9
  in fostering, V3.27
Family Health Service Authorities (FHSAs), WT.19, WT.20, V8.9
Family Law Reform Act, supervision orders, V7.42
Family Law Reform Act (1969), V1.42, V1.43, V7.36
  wardship, V7.38
Family Law Reform Act (1987), V2.71, V6.3, V7.35–6
family link schemes, V3.39, V4.41
  for children with disabilities, V6.33
family links
  with child in care, PP.9, CP.22
  of children looked after by local authority, V4.39
  for looked after children, V3.3
  preservation of, PP.8
  through care placements, CP.27
family proceedings, WT.122
  and adoption, V9.2
  local authority investigation of child's circumstances, V1.62–3
  meaning, V1.12–13
  welfare principles, V1.2
Family Proceedings Courts, WT.1
  Clerks, V7.16
Family Proceedings Courts (Children Act 1989) Rules (1991), V7.54–77
  application to commence, V7.57–8
  confidentiality, V7.68–9
  evidence, V7.66–7
  forms, V7.71–2
  guardian ad litem, V7.61–3
  hearing, V7.67–8

parties, V7.59–60
respondents and notice, V7.73–5
secure accomodation, V7.69
service, V7.60–1
solicitor for child, V7.63–4
welfare officer, V7.64
Family Rights Group model agreement, WT.42
family support, CP.39, V2.8
  for children in care and afterwards, CP.22
  local authorities, V2.3
  package, V6.18
  services, V2.1, V6.16
  social services, V2.8
father, parental responsibility, V2.71–2, V6.3
feelings of child, V1.20
financial assistance
  awareness of, V4.111
  purposes for which disregarded, V4.111
  young people leaving care, V4.110–11
financial problems, CP.11
financial provision for children, V1.19
financial skills
  and knowledge, V4.108
  preparation for leaving care, V3.98
fines, imposition, V4.19
fire
  department in registration of daycare services, V2.51
  drill and alarm tests at independent boarding schools, V5.10
  precautions in children's homes, V4.28
  safety, V2.81–2
first aid
  skills for foster parents, V8.17
  training, V2.35
food
  deprivation, V4.17–18, V8.13
  hygiene, V2.35–6, V2.82–3
  preparation, V4.5, V4.26, V4.27
Food Safety Act (1990), V2.82
foster care, V2.21, V3.22–3, V3.23
  access to parents, CP.24
  and adoption, V3.29
  age of children, CP.55
  age of own children, CP.30–2
  agreement, V3.30–1
  behaviour problems of children, CP.49
  breakdown rates, CP.67
  by relatives, CP.27
  children with special needs, V3.25
  child's history of abuse or neglect, CP.7
  classification, CP.59
  data on movement of children, CP.57
  family links, CP.26
  independent agency, V3.42
  limits on numbers, V3.34–5, V7.43, V8.5
  long-term, CP.67
  permanence through, CP.23
  permanent, CP.68
  professional for adolescents, CP.67
  protection of children in, WT.33–4
  publicity, V3.24
  rates and ethnic origin, CP.16
  and respite care, V6.34
  service, V2.7
  short-stay placements, CP.56
  short-term, CP.67
  specialist schemes, V6.36
  task-centred, CP.56
  teenage placements, CP.55
  teenage with similar aged children, CP.32
  termination, V8.15
  transition period, V3.28
  visits of parents, V3.66

written agreements, CP.49
foster care, private, V6.37, V8.1
  accomodation, V8.8
  after care, V8.24–5
  appeals, V8.26
  arranging placement of children, V8.5
  changes of circumstances, V8.15
  changes to arrangements, V8.16
  child development, V8.6
  and childminding, V8.30–1
  children in need, V8.4–5
  circumcision, V8.19–20
  communications, V8.11
  consent to medical examination or treatment, V8.18
  contact with child's family, V8.10
  cultural practices, V8.19–20
  death of child, V8.15
  declaration of suitability, V8.41
  definitions, V8.2–3
  diet for child, V8.13
  disqualification from, V8.3, V8.14, V8.46–50
  disturbed behaviour, V8.17
  duration, V8.6
  education of child, V8.9
  emergency, V8.14, V8.16
  emigration of child, V8.27–8
  enquiries about, V8.31
  ethnicity, V8.12, V8.13
  families abroad, V8.28
  financial arrangements, V8.7–8
  health of child, V8.8–9, V8.17
  household relationships, V8.12
  immigration, V8.27
  international aspects, V8.27–9
  language of child, V8.11
  legislative provisions, V8.2–3
  medical examination of child, V8.19
  medical history of child, V8.18
  nationality, V8.27
  nature of care, V8.31
  notification, V8.26
  notification of other persons involved, V8.16
  number of places, V8.31
  offences, V8.3, V8.25–6
  parental duty, V8.16
  parental visits, V8.13
  placements, V8.30
  premises, V8.4
  preparation for, V8.17
  prohibitions, V8.3, V8.4, V8.25
  provisions, V6.33
  purpose, V8.6
  refusal to allow visits, V8.24
  registration, V8.26
  registration of child with GP, V8.18
  religious practices, V8.19–20
  reports by local authority, V8.23
  requirements, V8.4
  rights of natural parent, V8.24
  seeing child alone, V8.23
  self-worth, V8.7
  sibling contact, V8.10
  statutory requirements, V8.3–5
  transitional arrangements, V7.43
  unsatisfactory care, V8.23–4
  visits to, V8.1
  welfare of child, V8.1, V8.3, V8.4, V8.6–7, V8.17–22, V8.24
  wishes of child, V8.10–11
foster care, private and local authority
  approach, V8.26–7
  enquiries, V8.11
  family placements, V8.30

notification, V8.3, V8.14–17
  records, V8.29
  visits, V8.22–3
foster carers see foster parents
Foster Children Act (1980), V8.1
foster families, drop out rate, CP.49
foster homes
  number of children in, V3.34–5, V7.43, V8.5
  suitability for children with disabilities, V6.36–7
foster parents, V3.31
  advice for, V8.9–10
  applicants, V3.24–7
  approval, V3.28–9
  in armed services, V3.40
  assessment, V3.24–7
  assessment of relatives and family friends as, V3.27
  communication with parents and authorities, V3.35
  complaints procedure, V3.32, V3.110
  confidentiality, V3.36
  contact with children being looked after, V3.66
  continuing relationship, V3.96, V4.106
  custodianship orders, V7.36
  discipline and sanctions, V3.27, V6.37, V8.13
  education attitudes, V8.13
  ethnic origins, V3.11
  first aid skills, V8.17
  help after leaving care, V4.109
  independent services, CP.49
  information to, V3.35–6
  involvement with schools, V6.35–6
  life style, V3.26, V8.13
  local community links, V6.36
  notification of local authority, V8.14–17
  notification of serious occurrences, WT.36
  parenting capacity, V8.12
  partnership with local authority, V3.87
  police records, V8.12
  preparation, V3.36
  public liability insurance, V8.9
  recruitment, V3.23–4
  recruitment for children with disabilities, V6.35–6
  refuges for children at risk, V4.130, V4.131–2
  relationship with child, V8.9
  relationship with child's parents, V8.11
  relationships with social workers, CP.49–50
  religious expectations, V8.12
  review, V3.29–30
  section 8 orders, V1.14
  selection, CP.56
  suitability, V8.9, V8.11–13
  support, CP.56, V3.31–2, V6.36
  termination of approval, V3.29–30
  training, CP.56, V3.31–2, V6.36
  views in after-care policy, V4.102
  views on preparation for leaving care, V3.93
  wishing to adopt, V9.8
foster parents, private
  parental responsibiity, V8.6
  responsibilities, V8.5–6
Foster Placement (Children) Regulations (1991), V3.22, V3.131–42
foster placements, V2.1–2
  agreement, V3.35
  for children with disabilities, V6.35–7
  child's needs, V3.33
  child's views, V3.33–4
  choice, V3.33–4

  continuity, V3.33
  disrupted, V3.41, V8.24
  educational continuity for children with disabilities, V6.35
  ending, V3.40–1
  financial arrangements, V3.36
  immediate, V3.37–8
  inter agency working, V3.41–2
  introduction of child, V3.36
  long term with siblings, CP.29–30
  outside England and Wales, V3.39–40
  overlap of regulations with children in care, V3.48
  preparation for, V3.36
  principles, PP.16
  records, V3.42
  with relatives, CP.67
  short-term, V3.38–9
  with siblings, CP.28
  supervision, V3.36–7
  visiting child, V3.36–7, V3.38
  visits, V3.36–7, V3.43
  voluntary organisations, V3.43–4
  welfare of child placed by voluntary organisation, V3.44
fostering allowance, V9.8
  enhancements, V9.14
fostering limit, V3.34–5, V7.43, V8.5
  transitional arrangements, V7.43
  usual, V3.110
Foundation for Womens Health Research and Development (FORWARD), V8.20
frustrated access conditions, V1.46
further education
  for children in homes, V4.23
  financial assistance, V4.111
  unqualified young people, V3.106
  for young people with disabilities, V3.105, V4.105
Further Education Councils, V6.48

G

GALRO panel, V7.3–4, V7.48, V7.50
  administration, V7.4–6
  appointment of members, V7.9–14
  committee, V7.6–8
  managers, V7.3, V7.5
  membership, V7.10–11
  size, V7.4
  temporary arrangements with neighbouring panels, V7.12
GALRO service
  appointment process, V7.11
  budget, V7.9
  case allocations, V7.14–17
  charges, V7.4
  communications, V7.21
  complaints boards, V7.20–1, V7.49, V7.50
  financial monitoring, V7.18
  flexibility, V7.4
  management arrangements, V7.3–9
  monitoring, V7.51
  professionalism, V7.18
  re-charging arrangements, V7.4
  record of appointment of members, V7.14
GALROs
  access to local authority records, V7.17
  in adoption proceedings, V7.15
  allowances, V7.8–9
  annual report, V7.19
  appointment, V7.49

avoidance of bias, V7.10–11
case allocation, V7.4, V7.17
confidentiality of records, V7.17
data collection and analysis, V7.18
eligibility criteria, V7.11
for emergency protection orders, V7.16
expenses, V7.8–9, V7.51
fees, V7.8–9, V7.51
functions, V7.16
immediate suspension, V7.13–14
inability to carry out functions, V7.13
induction training, V7.19
information technology use, V7.17
initial selection, V7.15
interviewing, V7.12
job description, V7.12
legal representation, V7.9
letter of appointment, V7.12
monitoring, V7.17–18
personal knowledge of child, V7.11
rates of payment, V7.8
reappointment, V7.12–13
records, V7.17, V7.18
recruitment, V7.11
representative on GALRO Panel Committee,
  V7.8
review, V7.18–19
social work qualifications, V7.11
specialist expertise requirements, V7.20
termination of appointment, V7.13–14, V7.49
training, V7.19–20, V7.51
types of proceedings, V7.14–15
unfitness, V7.13
see also guardians ad litem
gay men and women, V3.97, V3.98
gay young people
  needs and concerns, V4.107
  self-esteem development, V4.107
General Medical Council, WT.12
general practitioner
  assessment of young people with
    disabilities, V6.51
  for children in care, V4.20
  registration of privately fostered child, V8.18
  role in child protection, WT.20
good child care practice, V3.91
  principles, PP.1, PP.7–15, PP.18–20
grandparents
  party status, V1.26
  section 8 orders, V1.14
grants for young people leaving care, V4.111
grievance procedure, V4.80
grounds at independent boarding schools,
  V5.9
growth charts, CP.8
guardian
  appointment, V1.7–8
  appointment of father, V1.6
guardian ad litem, WT.122, V1.3, V7.2
  access to records, WT.71
  appointment, V4.126, V7.2
  in care and supervision orders, V1.20
  in child assessment orders, V1.47
  in child protection work, WT.16
  for children with disabilities, V6.46–7
  GALRO service, V7.2
  and independent visitor, V4.95
  legal framework, WT.71
  number on panel, V7.9–10
  Official Solicitor as, V7.16
  response to court demands, V7.3
  and restriction of liberty, V4.118, V4.120
  role, V7.2
  timing of proceedings, V1.27

Guardians ad Litem and Reporting Officers
  (Panels) Regulations (1991), V7.48–53
guardianship, V1.5, V2.72–3
  disclaimer, V1.8–9
  revocation, V1.8–9
  termination, V1.8–9
  transitional provisions, V2.73
Guardianship Act (1973), V6.3
Guernsey
  care orders, V7.31
  transfer of care orders, V7.79
guesting, CP.47
guidance
  boarding-out, PP.3
  for children in need, V6.5
  distribution to practitioners, CP.130–2
  documents and circulars, PP.2
  focus range and depth, PP.3–6
  status of, PP.2–3

H

haemophilia, V4.20
halfway accomodation
  for after-care, V4.113, V4.114
  voluntary services, V4.112
harbouring children, exemption from
  prosecution, V4.130
hard to reach groups of children, V6.17
harm, V1.20, V1.23–4
  assessment and examination, V1.31
  child assessment orders, V1.45
  definition, V1.24
  long-term and cumulative, V1.46
  and parenting, V1.24
harm, likelihood of significant, V1.25, V1.26
  local authorities' responsibilities, V2.12
harm, significant, WT.126
  definition, WT.49
  police powers, V1.60–1
health, V2.35
  carers, V3.52
  children in care, CP.7
  definition, V1.24
  education in schools, WT.22
  minor shortcomings in care, V1.25
  and placement of children arrangements,
    V4.43, V4.43–4
  problems at independent boarding schools,
    V5.9
  publications, V6.63
  requirements of young people with
    disabilities, V4.105
  review of children's cases, V3.85
  surveillance programmes, WT.19, WT.20,
    V8.17
health assessment, WT.118, V4.19
  placement of children, V3.8
health authority
  accomodation, V4.36
  restriction of liberty of children accomodated
    by, V4.121
health care, V4.19–20
  of child in private fostering, V8.8–9
  of children in accomodation, V3.7–9
  ethnic minority groups, V3.8
  independent boarding schools, V5.9, V5.10
  major needs, V6.28
  needs and placement of children in care with
    parents, V3.50
  private, WT.20
  specialist needs, V6.29

health records, V4.20–1
  parent-held, V6.15
health and safety
  conditions, V2.39
  policy at independent boarding schools,
    V5.10
  in registration of day care services, V2.51
  requirements for day care providers,
    V2.83–4
Health and Safety at Work etc Act (1974),
  V2.83
health services
  adult, V4.105
  child protection work, WT.17–20
  co-ordinators, WT.18
  records, WT.18
  role for children with disabilities, V6.27–9
Health Services Act (1984), 65
Health and Social Services and Social Security
  Adjudications Act (1983), CP.46
health visitor, WT.18
  information on foster parents, V8.12
hearing aids, V6.36
hearings, interval between, V1.27
heating at independent boarding schools, V5.9
help provision planning, PP.7–8
helplines, WT.23
  telephone, V5.13
Her Majesty' Inspector of Schools (HMI),
  independent boarding schools, V5.3–4, V5.14
High Court, V1.2
  appeals, V1.3
  family proceedings, V1.21
  inherent jurisdiction, V1.42–3
  Official Solicitor as guardian ad litem, V7.16
  wardship and inherent jurisdiction, V4.127–8
HIV positivity, V4.20–1
holding, V4.17
holiday schemes, V2.17, V2.79
Home Start Consultancy, V6.19
home on trial placement, CP.9, CP.21
  change of children in home, CP.32
  classification for support and supervision,
    CP.58
  involvement of relatives, CP.27
  parental participation, CP.42
  planning, CP.64
  protected children, CP.71
  with siblings, CP.29
  social worker support, CP.47
  social workers' problems, CP.44–5
  success, CP.66–7
  support required, CP.66–7
Home-Start schemes, V2.27
homeless
  family accomodation, V6.17
  proportion having left care, V4.114
  vulnerability, V4.113
homelessness, CP.11
  young people leaving care, V3.103, V3.104
Homelessness Advice Service, V3.102, V4.112
homework facilities, V4.22–3
hospices
  accomodation, V6.39
  children's, V6.28
hospital staff, WT.18–19
housing
  needs of young people leaving care, V3.104
  voluntary services, V4.112
  young people with disabilities, V3.94, V4.104
Housing Act (1985), V3.103, V4.113
housing associations, V3.103, V3.104
  accomodation for after-care, V4.113
housing authorities, V2.20

range of services for children with disabilities, V6.53–4
role in after-care, V3.103–4, V4.113–14
hygiene
  in food preparation, V4.27
  standards at independent boarding schools, V5.10

I

implementation of act, V1.4
implications of Children Act (1989), PP.1
incest offenders, WT.38
Income Support, V4.111, V4.117
independent boarding schools, V4.3–4
  accomodation definition, V5.4
  accomodation standards, V5.8–9
  accountability of proprietor, V5.6
  accreditation systems, V5.3
  authorised person for inspections, V5.19
  behaviour at, V5.11–12
  best practice use, V5.3
  care of mentally disordered and handicapped, V5.18
  child abuse at, V5.6–7
  child protection procedures, WT.35
  children with disabilities at, V6.40
  communication with other agencies, V5.3
  complaints procedure, V5.13, V5.15
  corporal punishment, V5.12
  discipline at, V5.11–12
  duties, V5.1
  exclusion from Act, V5. 2
  frequency of SSD visits, V5.14
  governors, V5.2
  health care facilities, V5.9, V5.10
  health problems, V5.9
  HMI inspection, V5.3–4, V5.14
  hygiene standards, V5.10
  inspection of children, V5.19, V5.21–2
  inspection of premises, V5.19–20, V5.21
  level of care, V5.5
  lifestyle, V5.10
  management, V5.5
  notification of health matters, V5.10
  personal relations at, V5.11–12
  proprietor, V5.2, V5.15, V5.17
  punishments, V5.12
  records, V5.20
  records inspection, V5.19–20, V5.22
  registering as children's home, V5.17
  religious and cultural ethos, V5.11
  reports of SSD visits, V4.14–15
  rewards and sanctions, V5.12
  safety procedures, V5.10
  Secretary of State's inspection powers, V5.18
  separation from family, V5.3
  SSD inspection, WT.35, V5.14
  SSD responsibilities, V5.2, V5.3
  staff liaison with SSD, V5.4
  statement of principles, V5.5
  training needs of staff, V5.6
  transitional arrangements, V7.43–4
  welfare of children in, V5.2–3, V5.17–18
  see also staff at independent boarding schools
independent living
  questionnaires, CP.90–105
  schemes, V6.49
  training, CP.10
  transition to, CP9–13, V4.101

independent person
  appointment, V3.116
  appointment for representations procedure, V4.82
  consideration of complaint, V3.118
  decision, V3.118–19
  panel meeting, V3.119
  for representations procedure, V1.18–19, V3.115–16, V4.81–2, V4.84
independent schools
  nursery units, V2.78
  vetting staff, V4.9
Independent Schools Tribunal, V5.15
independent visitor, V3.71
  advice to child, V3.77–8
  advisory role, V4.94
  advocacy, V3.78–9
  aftercare, V3.99
  appointment, V3.71, V3.75, V4.92–3
  assessment, V4.91
  befriending, V3.78, V4.94
  carer's anxieties, V3.74
  for children with disabilities in residential care, V6.31–2
  children for whom appointed, V3.72, V4.89
  child's preference, V4.90
  child's views, V3.73
  continuing relationships after care, V4.96
  in court proceedings, V4.95
  definition, V3.71–2, V4.88
  duration of relationship, V3.73
  duty to appoint, V4.88
  effectiveness, V3.74, V4.91
  expenses, V3.79, V4.96
  function, V4.93–5
  help after leaving care, V4.109
  help to child in serious situations, V4.95–6
  inappropriate behaviour, V4.93
  interests of child, V4.89
  meetings with local authority, V3.78, V4.95
  outings with child, V4.94
  pool of persons, V3.73–4, V4.90
  records, V4.91
  recruitment, V3.73–5, V4.90–2
  regulations, V4.178–9
  relationship with carers, V4.91
  relationship duration, V4.90
  relatives as, V3.73, V4.90
  resignation, V3.75–6
  review of appointment, V3.75–6, V4.92
  in review of children's cases, V3.85, V4.60, V4.62, V4.63
  role and function, V3.76–8, V4.93–5
  selection, V3.72–3, V4.89–90
  support, V3.74–5, V4.91–2
  termination of appointment, V3.75–6, V4.92–3
  training, V3.74, V4.91–2
  visiting, V3.77, V4.93–4
  welfare of child, V4.93
individual protection cases
  abuse by stranger, WT.36–7
  child assessment orders, WT.29
  children in foster care, WT.33–4
  children living away from home, WT.33
  comprehensive assessment, WT.31–2
  court action, WT.25–6
  decision making, WT.31
  extra-familial abuse, WT.36
  focus on child, WT.30
  immediate protection, WT.27–8
  initial assessment, WT.28–31
  investigation, WT.28–31
  notification of serious occurrences, WT.36

  planning, WT.31–2
  planning investigation, WT.27–8
  referral and recognition, WT.27
  in residential care, WT.34–6
  staff selection for interviewing, WT.29
  stages of work, WT.26–7
  strategy discussion, WT.28
  timing, WT.31
  written plan, WT.32–3
individuals, children and their families as, PP.7–12
information
  exchange, WT.11–12
  sharing, WT.17
  systems, V2.8
information technology
  aids, V6.15
  for GALRO monitoring, V7.17
injunction, WT.122
  transitional arrangements, V7.38
injury to self or other people, V4.123, V4.124
inspection
  of children at independent boarding schools, V5.19–20, V5.21–2
  of premises at independent boarding schools, V5.19–20, V5.21
Inspection of Premises, Children and Records (Independent Schools) Regulations (1991), V5.21–2
Inspection Unit, V2.64
insurance, public liability, V8.9
integration and special health care needs, V6.28
inter-agency case conferences, complaints, V4.76
inter-agency co-operation, WT.5, V1.22
  geographical boundaries, WT.39
  responsibility for, WT.5
  sharing information, WT.17
inter-agency investigation, in organised abuse cases, WT.39
inter-agency liaison, V3.88
inter-agency plan, WT.122
inter-agency training, WT.7, WT.17, WT.54
inter-agency work, legal constraints and context, WT.10–11
Interpretation Act (1978), V7.41
interviewing
  child witnesses, WT.53
  joint, WT.53
  recording in child protection cases, WT.30
Isle of Man
  care orders, V7.30–1
  transfer of care orders, V7.79
  transfer of recovery orders, V7.80

J

Jersey, care orders, V7.31
Job Centre, V4.116
jobs for pocket money, V4.20
Joint Lord Chancellor's Guidance/Home Office Guidance (Home Office Circular No 45/91), V7.114–120
judicial review, WT.123
juvenile offenders, V3.31
  cautioning, V1.71
  recognisance orders, V1.75
  residence requirement in criminal supervision orders, V1.73–4
  reviews of cases, V1.75
  social enquiry report, V1.74

juvenile offending, V1.4, V1.69
  crime prevention, V1.69–71
  diversion from prosecution, V1.69–71
juveniles
  absconding from local authority
    accomodation, V1.77
  arrest by responsible person, V1.77
  arrested and detained, V7.45–6
  remands, V7.46

K

key worker, WT.42, WT.43, WT.123, V6.11
  child protection register, WT.107
  system, V4.11–12
kitchen facilities, V4.25

L

language
  development of commonly spoken, V4.23
  privately fostered children, V8.11
  sign, V8.11
latchkey children, V2.29
laundry in children's homes, V4.15–16
law, comprehensiveness of, PP.1
Law Society' Child Care Panel, V4.126
leaflets, representations procedure, V4.78
learning difficulties
  identification, V6.24
  responsibilities of Further Education
    Councils, V6.48
learning disability
  NHS provision, V6.33
  teams, V6.28
leaving care *see* after-care; care leavers;
 preparation for leaving care
Legal Aid Act 1988 (Children Act 1989) Order
 (1991), V7.121–2
Legal Aid Act (1988), V4.126
Legal Aid in Criminal and Care Proceedings
 (Costs) (Amendment) (No. 3) Regulations
 (1991), V7.128–9
Legal Aid in Criminal and Care Proceedings
 (General)(Amendment)(No. 2) Regulations
 (1991), V7.128–9
legal aid entitlement, V4.125, V4.126
legal department in registration of daycare
 services, V2.50
legal framework, WT.63–71
  care proceedings, WT.66–7
  child assessment orders, WT.69–70
  contact with children in care, WT.67–8
  duties of local authorities in relation to
    children looked after by them, WT.64
  duty to investigate, WT.65
  emergency procedures, WT.68–9
  family assistance orders, WT.70
  general principles, WT.63
  guardian ad litem, WT.71
  orders, WT.70
  preventive measures, WT.63–4
  provision of accomodation, WT.64
  representation procedure, WT.65
  review of cases, WT.65
legal representation
  High Court hearings, V4.128
  in restriction of liberty, V4.126
liberty, restriction of, V1.4, V4.18–19, V4.118,
 V4.126, V7.33
  appeals, V4.127

applications to court, V4.125
at independent boarding schools, V5.12–13
children accomodated by health and
  education authorities, V4.121
for children with disabilities, V6.39
children excluded from provisions, V4.123
children looked after by local authorities,
  V4.120–1
court authority, V4.125
criteria for, V1.66–7, V4.123
definition, V4.120
detained children, V4.123–4
guardians ad litem appointment, V4.126
legal representation, V4.126
maximum period, V4.126–7
in mental nursing homes, V4.121–2
minimum age, V4.122
modified criteria, V1.67
in nursing homes, V4.121–2
registered children's homes, V4.121
remanded children, V4.123–4
in residential care homes, V4.121–2
reviews, V4.128–9
secure accomodation notification, V4.124
statement of policy, V4.122
statutory framework, V4.119–20
time restriction, V4.124–5
voluntary homes, V4.121
without court authority, V4.124–5
library
  and information services for children with
    disabilities, V6.53–4
  in registration of daycare services, V2.50
life threatening conditions, V6.28–9
  accomodation for children, V6.39
  publications on care of children, V6.63
Lifestory books, V6.15
linguistic background
  foster parents, V3.26
  in placement of children arrangements,
    V4.43, V4.46–7
  in welfare of child, CP.5
linguistic needs, and placement of children in
 care with parents, V3.51
living
  environment of children with disabilities,
    V6.36–7
  expenses, V3.89
local authority
  access to child, V1.63
  access to records, PP.12–13
  acquisition of parental responsibility, V2.1
  adoption counselling services, V9.19, V9.20
  advice and assistance, V1.77–8
  agreement of plans for children in care,
    V3.17
  application for care and supervision orders,
    WT70, V1.21, V1.22
  appointment of guardians, V1.8
  appointment of independent visitor, V4.88
  assessment of need, V2.6–7
  assistance to young people leaving care,
    V3.101–2, V4.116
  availability of services, V2.8
  care, V1.21
  charging for services, V2.13–14
  children with disabilities, V2.9–10
  children in need in privte fostering, V8.5
  children in other establishments, V2.13
  children with special needs, V1.39
  co-operation between departments, PP.12
  co-operation in day care provision, V2.26–7
  co-operation with enquiries, V1.64
  co-operation with parents, WT.2, V4.74

co-ordination responsibilities, V2.3–4
community care, V2.3–4
complaints about, V4.76
complaints about GALRO service, V7.20
complaints board for GALROs, V7.13
comprehensibility of communications, PP.13
confidentiality of records, PP.12–13
contact arrangements for children in care,
  V3.63
contact decisions, V4.70–1, V4.72
courts arrangements, V1.78
day care services, V2.1, V2.4, V2.15–18
differences between, CP.74–5
discharge or variation of orders, V1.33
duties, PP.5, WT.64
duty to investigate, WT.65, WT.79–81,
  WT.121, V1.62–4
education for looked after and accomodated
  children, V3.10
education matters, V1.63
eligibility criteria for GALROs, V7.11
emergency protection order, V1.53, V1.54,
  V1.63
employees as guardians ad litem, V7.10
employment of GALRO Panel Manager,
  V7.5
enquiries, V1.63
enquiries about suitability of foster parents,
  V8.11
establishment of GALRO panel, V7.3–4
facilities for juveniles, V1.69–70
and families, V1.1
family centres, V2.18–20
family support services, V2.1, V2.3
financial help for care leavers, CP.61,
  V3.101–2
financial help to foster parents, V8.7
foster parents, V1.12
GALRO's expenses, V7.8
housing provision, V4.113–14
identification of children in need, WT.63,
  V2.1, V2.2
independent visitors' meetings, V3.78, V4.95
information services, V2.30–1
information systems, V2.8
and inherent jurisdiction of High Court,
  V1.42–3
inter-agency arrangements, V3.19, V4.55
liaison, V3.88
inter-departmental collaboration, V2.2
investigation, V1.2
investigation of abuse and neglect, WT.9–10
Juvenile crime prevention, V1.69–70
juveniles remanded to accomodation,
  V1.66–7, V1.68
legal advice, V1.22–3
legal responsibility, WT.9
liaison with police, V1.62
meeting needs of children, V2.7–8
officer support, V2.77
parental role, V4.97
parents wishes, PP.5
parents working with, V1.50
partnership in decision making, V2.11–12
partnership with parents, WT.1, V3.87
placement of children in independent
  boarding schools, V5.15–16
placement patterns, CP.61
planning services, PP.13
powers of investigation in child abuse, V1.44
premises for private fostering, V8.4
principles of good work with children and
  families, PP.12
privately fostered children, V8.3

prohibition powers in private fostering, V8.25
promotion of contact with child, V1.39
promotion of contact with children not looked after, V3.63
provision of accomodation, V1.76–7
publicising services, V2.13
records of private fostering, V8.29
refusal of access, V1.63
refusal of contact with child, V1.38
remands to accomodation, V1.75–6
reports on private foster home visits, V8.23
representation procedure, WT.65, V3.108
representative on GALRO Panel Committee, V7.7
residence requirement in criminal supervision orders, V1.73
resource allocation priorities, V2.2, V2.3
responsibilities, V1.22
responsibility in care orders, V1.35–6
review of children in secure accomodation, V4.128–9
review duty for daycare, V2.65–6
right of appeal, V1.3
section 8 orders, V1.14–15
statutory duties of investigation of harm to children, WT.15
strategic planning, CP.59–62
support of child leaving care, V4.97
support of parents, V2.7
termination of access, CP.61
transitional arrangements for maintenance contributions, V7.41
visits to children's homes, V4.32, V4.144–5
visits to private foster homes, V8.22–3
visits to voluntary organisation foster placements, V3.43
voluntary organisations, V2.27–8
vountary arrangements for looking after child, V3.2, V3.4–5
welfare of privately fostered children, V8.4
welfare responsibilities, V2.3, V2.5
wishes of child, WT.1–2, PP.5
written policies for leaving care, V3.92–3
see also looked after children
local authority accomodation
  for child, PP.8, V1.63
  in criminal supervision orders, V1.73
  provision, WT.64, V1.39, V2.10–11, V2.20–2
  provision by voluntary agreement, V4.40–1
  suitability for private fostering, V8.8
local authority after-care, V2.12–13, V3.87
  from private fostering, V8.24
  powers and duties, V3.88–9, V4.98–100
  responsibilities, V3.100
local authority notification
  of child leaving care, V3.90, V3.91
  policy, V8.16–17
  system for private fostering, V8.3, V8.14–17, V8.16
local authority policy
  on financial assistance, V3.101–2
  and guidance to practitioners, CP.62–3, CP.75
  for housing needs of young people leaving care, V3.104
  issues, V2.2–3
  on leaving care, V4.102–3
  research in development, V2.3
local authority services
  from other agencies, V2.8
  planning for individual child, V2.7
  provision, WT.9
  provision for children with disabilities, V6.13
  regulatory function in day care, V2.26

Local Authority Social Services Act (1970), V2.25, V3.108, V4.74
Local Commissioner, V4.79
local education authority (LEA)
  accomodation for children with disabilities, V6.39–40
  children with disabilities in residential schools, V6.40
  education supervision orders, V6.25–6, V7.22, V7.23
  involvement with SSDs for children with disabilities, V6.21
  notification of placement, V3.10
  notification to SSDs of special educational needs, V6.22–3
  policies on education supervision orders, V7.23
  range of services for children with disabilities, V6.53
  in registration of daycare services, V2.50
  report to court for education supervision order, V7.24–5
  restriction of liberty of children accomodated by, V4.121
  review duty for daycare, V2.65–6
  supervising officer for education supervision orders, V7.26
  in transition to adulthood of disabled young person, V6.49
  transitional arrangements for accomodation, V7.43
  use of education supervision orders, V7.29
Local Government (Access to Information) Act (1985), V3.121, V4.87
Local Government Act (1972), V3.19
Local Government Act (1974), Local Commissioner, V4.79
Local Government and Housing Act (1989), V6.57
local procedural handbooks, WT.8
  content, WT.111–12
  format, WT.112
lodgings
  vetting, V4.8
  voluntary services, V4.112
loneliness, CP.11, CP.34
looked after children, V2.5, V3.2, V3.2–4, V4.38, V4.38–40, V7.33
  accomodation provision by voluntary agreement, V3.4–5, V3.6
  children from abroad, V8.40
  children living abroad, V8.37–40
  duties towards, WT.64
  education, V3.9–10
  family links, V3.3
  independent visitors, V3.71
  participation in decisions, V3.4, V3.6
  partnership of responsible authority with parents, V3.4
  protection of public, V3.3
  review of cases, WT.65
  review of children accomodated by local authority, V4.38
  welfare, V3.2–3

M

magistrates' family proceedings courts, V1.2, V1.21
mail for children at independent boarding schools, V5.10
maintenance contributions by local authorities, transitional arrangements, V7.41

Makaton, V6.32, V6.36, V8.11
managers, distribution of guidance, CP.130–2
Managing Behaviour, V8.13
Manual of Practice Guidance for GALRO Panel Managers, V7.3
Manual of Practice Guidance for Guardians ad Litem and Reporting Officers, V7.3
Maria Colwell Report, CP.8
Matrimonial Causes Act (1973), V1.16, V1.17, V7.35
  custody under, V7.39
  financial provisions, V1.19
  supervision orders, V7.42
Matrimonial Homes Act (1983), V1.17
Matrimonial Proceedings (Magistrates' Court Act)(1960), V7.36
meal
  preparations, V4.25, V4.26, V4.27
  times, V4.25–6
medical assessment, WT.117
medical and dental treatment, withholding, V4.18
medical examination, V4.19
  children before and during placement, V4.44
  children in care, CP.8
  consent, V3.9, V4.44–5
  consent of child, WT.63
  consent of children with disabilities, V6.46
  consent in private fostering, V8.18
  emergency protection orders, V1.59
  placement of children, V3.8, V3.9
medical history
  children in care, CP.8
  of children to be fostered, V8.9
medical information, WT.12
medical records, children in care, CP.8
medical treatment
  consent, V3.9, V4.21, V4.44–5
  consent of child, WT.63
  consent of children with disabilities, V6.46
  consent in private fostering, V8.18
  and placement of children arrangements, V4.43
  staff role, V4.21
medication, V4.20
  administration, V4.21
mental handicap, V1.15
Mental Health Act (1983), V8.3
  children detained under, V4.123
Mental Health Service, Child and Adolescent, WT.19–20
mental nursing homes, V4.36
  for children with disabilities, V6.38
  restriction of liberty, V4.121–2
  transitional arrangements, V7.43
menus, V4.25, V4.26
midwife, WT.18
  designated senior, WT.121
monitoring, WT.123
mother, parental responsibility, V2.71–2
multi-cultural society, PP.1
multi-ethnic society, PP.1

N

nannies, V2.45, V2.79
National Assistance Act (1948), V2.1, V6.5, V6.7
National Bureau for Students with Disabilities, V6.50
National Curriculum, access to by children with disabilities, V6.21
National Health Service Act (1977), WT.65, V2.1

National Nursery Examination Board, V2.33
National Society for the Prevention of Cruelty to Children see NSPCC
National Vocational Qualifications, V2.33
need, children in, WT.119, V6.5–6
  accomodation, V2.8
  aids and adaptations to house, V6.6
  assessment procedures, V6.9
  classification, CP.58–9
  co-ordination of services, V6.7–8
  collaborative work with, V6.7
  contact and re-unification with family, V2.13
  day care services, V2.15–18
  definition, V2.5–8
  emergency protection, WT.81–2
  family support services, V6.5, V6.16
  identification by local authorities, WT.63
  identification of, V2.1, V2.2, V6.6
  living away from home, V2.12
  living with families, V2.10
  meeting needs, V2.7–8
  private fostering, V8.4–5
  service planning for individual child, V2.7
  services for, V6.5–6
  transport for, V6.6
  welfare promotion and safeguards, V3.1
needs, V1.20
  assessment, V2.6–7
  basic, PP.7
  consideration of, PP.7
  of individual child, PP.4
neglect, WT.48
  entitlement to protection from, PP.7
  investigation, WT.9–10
NEWPIN, V2.17
NHS
  children living in provision, V6.29
  role for children in need, V6.7
  short-term care, V6.33
  trust accomodation for children with disabilities, V6.39–40
NHS and Community Care Act (1990), V2.64, V6.9–10, V6.11
  amendments to Act in, V7.91–5
non-parental care for children, V2.30
Northern Ireland
  care orders, V7.30–1
  transfer of care orders, V7.79
  transfer of recovery orders, V7.80
NSPCC, WT.23, V1.21
  applications when juvenile subject to order, V1.75
  case responsibility, WT.31
  in child abuse cases, V4.33
  child protection conference, WT.41, WT.46
  child protection plan, WT.33
  in emergency protection orders, V1.53
  referrals, WT.27
  training, WT.53, WT.54
nurse, designated senior, WT.121
nurseries, transitional arrangements, V7.43
Nurseries and Child-Minders Regulation Act (1948), V2.62
nursery centres, combined, V2.79
nursery education, V2.24
  availability, V2.65–6
  combined with day care services, V2.44
  premises, V2.43–4
  private, V2.44–5
  quantity, V2.65–6
  staffing, V2.44
nursery schools, maintained, V2.78
nursery schools, private, V2.44–5, V2.78, V6.40

applications for registration, V8.34–5
registration and inspection fees, V8.36
nursing homes, V4.36
  for children with disabilities, V6.38
  restriction of liberty, V4.121–2
  transitional arrangements, V7.43
nursing information, WT.12

O

occupational therapist, V6.36
offence condition abolition, V1.71
offenders, social background, CP.6
offending, people at risk, V1.69, V1.70
Official Solicitor, WT.123, V1.7
  as guardian ad litem, V7.16
open access facilities, V2.48
opportunity groups, V6.19
orders, V1.9–12
  contact, V1.9, V1.11, V1.12
  court's duty when considering, V1.16–17
  parental responsibility, V1.6
  prohibited steps, V1.9, V1.11–12
  residence, 13, V1.9–11
  section 8, V1.9–15
  specific issue, V1.9, V1.12
out-of-school clubs, V2.17, V2.79, V3.24
outreach
  after-care services, CP.12–13
  work, V4.131
overseas trips, V1.10

P

paedophile rings, WT.38
Panel Committee of GALRO service, V7.6–8, V7.49, V7.50–1
  cost of administration, V7.8
  members, V7.7–8
  review system, V7.19
Panel Manager of GALRO service, V7.5–6
  appraisal system, V7.19
  complaints about service, V7.20
  consultation role, V7.6
  quality of service, V7.6
  selection of member, V7.15
paramountcy principle, WT.123
parent/toddler groups, V2.17–18
  for children with disabilities, V6.19
parentage, mixed race, CP.15
  care admissions of children, CP.35
  separation of siblings, CP.28
parental care, breakdown for child with disability, V6.44
parental contact
  barriers to, CP.120–3
  placement of child in care outside England and Wales, V3.60
  and placement of children arrangements, V4.43
parental control, child beyond, V1.24, V1.26
parental involvement
  with child in care, PP.9
  in continuing care plan, V4.101
  in day care services, V2.34–5
  in review meeting, V3.83–4
parental partnership
  in care of children with disabilities, V6.13, V6.14
  with carers, CP.39–41
  with local authority, V3.87

with local authority in placement arrangements, V4.40
  in placement of children arrangements, V4.53
  see also partnership with parents and carers
parental responsibility, WT.123, V1.1, V1.5, V2.71–6
  accomodation arrangements, V2.21–2
  in accomodation of children with disabilities, V6.30
  accomodation provision by voluntary agreement, V3.5, V4.41
  acquisition by local authorities, V2.1
  in adoption, V9.1
  allocation, V1.5–7
  appointment of guardians, V1.7–8
  arranging placement of children in private fostering, V8.5–6
  and care orders, V1.35, V1.36, V2.73–4
  child looked after by local authority, V3.2
  children in care, V2.75
  children with disabilities, V6.3–4
  and children living abroad, V8.39
  and consultation about review of children's cases, V4.60
  counselling, V2.23
  court order for, WT.1, V6.3, V6.4
  Criminal Justice Act (1991), V7.46
  delegation, V1.7
  education of child, V7.22
  and education supervision orders, V7.25
  in emergency protection order, V1.58, V2.73–4
  exercise of, V2.74, V6.4
  family assistance orders, V2.75–6
  father, V2.71–2
  guardian, V2.72–3
  infrequent contact with child, V4.89
  married parents, V1.5–7
  meaning, V1.5
  mother, V2.71–2
  not visiting child, V4.89
  notification duty of private fostering arrangements, V8.16
  order, V1.6
  pending proceedings, V7.35
  in placement of children arrangements, V1.6–17, V4.42
  placement of children in care with parents, V3.49
  and police protection, V1.62
  and private fostering, V8.4, V8.5
  private law orders, V2.76
  private proceedings, V2.75
  referral to local authority, V2.76
  and residence orders, V1.9–10, V2.73
  shared, V1.10
  sharing with local authority, V3.62
  specific restriction, V1.11–12
  in supervision orders, V1.40
  unmarried parents, V1.5–7
parental rights and duties, father where parents not married, V7.35–6
parenthood, V1.5
parenting, corporate, PP.11
Parentline, WT.23
parents
  access disputes, CP.26, CP.42
  attendance at review meetings, CP.51, V4.60, V4.61
  case conference attendance, CP.51
  co-operation with local authorities, V4.74
  co-operation in local authority accomodation provision, V2.11

communication with foster parents, V3.35
conflict of interests with child, WT.43
in consultation about review of children's cases, V4.60
consultation in care of children with disabilities, V6.13, V6.14
consultation in decision making, V2.11–12
contact with at independent boarding schools, V5.10
contact with children in care, V1.37, V3.61–3, V4.65–6, V4.67
contribution towards maintenance, V7.41
counselling, V2.23
counselling needs with children with disabilities, V6.24
day care needs, V2.30
disadvantage in court, 45
disadvantaged, CP.44
disagreement over contact, V4.72
failing to comply with direction of education supervision orders, V7.27
family links with child in care, PP.9
help and consideration, PP.8
helpful qualities in social workers, CP.47
as individuals, PP.8
informed choice of care, V8.-9
infrequent contact with child, V4.89
isolation and depression with children with disabilities, V6.19
links with children in care, CP.24
marginalising, CP.45
medical examination or treatment of children in placement, V4.45
not carers in placement of children in care with parents, V3.55–6
not visiting child, V4.89
notification duty of private fostering arrangements, V8.16
participation in home on trial placement, CP.42
placement of children with care orders, V3.45–7, V3.49
planning placement of children, V3.13
planning and review of child's case, V4.40
and private fostering, V8.4, V8.5
protection of children against, CP.44
reasonable care, V1.25
relationship with childminder, V2.46
removal of rights in education supervision orders, V7.25, V7.26
responsibility for child in private fostering, V8.6
in review of children's cases, V4.61, V4.62, V4.63
right of appeal, V1.3
right of appeal against education supervision orders, V7.28
rights, V2.38
social workers as agents, CP.51
support from local authorities, V2.7
support services, V2.22–3
transitional arrangements for placement with, V7.39
understanding of problems by social workers, CP.40–1
views in after-care policy, V4.102
views on preparation for leaving care, V3.93
visits to child in care, V4.68–9
visits to fostered children, V8.13
working partnership with, PP.8
parties to proceedings, WT.123–4
partnership with parents and carers, CP.39–41
barriers, CP.44–6
current studies, CP.42–3

DATA syndrome, CP.46
differences in perspective, CP.40
good practice and, CP.47–8
implications for policy and practice, CP.51
success in, CP.47–8
see also parental partnership
party status, V1.26–7, V1.34
peer groups, under fives, V2.29
peer interactions, V2.38–9
pending proceedings, V7.35
permanence movement, 23
permanency planning, WT.124
personal balance sheet for independent living, CP.90–105
personal development, young people with disabilities, V6.52
personal identity of child in care, PP.10
personal relations, at independent boarding schools, V5.11–12
personal requisites, V4.27–8
phased care, V3.39
for children with disabilities, V6.33
physical abuse, remedial service requirements of children, CP.34
physical injury to child, WT.48
physical searches, intimate, V4.19
place of safety, V9.1–2
orders and transitional arrangements, V1.80, V7.42
placement of children
access to records, V3.21
accomodation provision by voluntary agreement, V4.40–1
agencies involved, V3.13–14
agreements, V3.16–17, V4.52–3
already disadvantaged, CP.6–7
arrangements, V3.3–4, V4.38
assessment of needs, V3.14–15, V4.50–1
breakdown rate, CP.57
case records, V3.20
children looked after by local authority, V4.38–40
children subject to court order, V4.41
child's views, V3.12–13, V4.48–9
classification, CP.74
communication difficulties, V4.49, V4.51, V4.53–4
consultation, V3.12–14, V4.48, V4.49–50
contact with family, V3.65
contact implications, V4.68
contingency planning, V4.47
court orders, V3.5
cultural background, V4.46–7
decision making, CP.75, V3.15, V4.51
defining success, CP.66
education, V3.9–10, V4.45–6
ethnic origins, V3.11
ethnicity and outcome, CP.17
factors associated with breakdown, CP.68–9
family, V3.13
family involvement, V4.49
foster care, V3.22–32
health assessment, V3.8
health care, V3.7–9, V4.43–4
implementation of decisions, V4.54
implementation of plan, V3.18
information on, CP.54
inquiry, V3.12, V4.48
inter-agency arrangements, V4.55
leaving accomodation, V4.53
linguistic background, V3.11, V4.46–7, V4.49
local authority, V3.2–4
long-term out-of-home, PP.13

matching needs, strengths and resources, CP.132–3
medical examination and treatment, V3.8, V3.9, V4.43–5
monitoring support and supervision, V3.18, V4.54
notification of decisions, V4.53–4
notification of plan, V3.17–18
objectives, CP.49
outcomes, CP.17, CP.57, CP.75
outside England and Wales, V3.19, V4.55
over 16 years of age, V3.47
partnership with parents, V4.40, V4.53
patterns of local authorities, CP.61
permanent with siblings, CP.29
plan, V3.5–6, V3.15–16, V4.39–40, V4.41–2, V4.51–2
planning, V3.11–18
planning process, CP.64, CP.65–9, V4.47–54
preparation for leaving, V3.17
racial origin, V4.46–7
records, V3.14, V3.18, V3.19–21, V4.54, V4.55–7
records of consultation, V4.50
register, V3.20, V4.56
with relatives or friends, PP.8
religion, V3.11, V4.46–7
research, CP.1
review, V4.39–40, V4.41
review of establishments, PP.15
review of short-term, V4.59
risk assessment, CP.65–9
short pre-planned, V4.41
short-term, V3.5
siblings, V4.42
social conditions before, CP.6
statistics, CP.74
statutory responsibility, V3.70
support by agencies, PP.14
task-centred, CP.74
voluntary agreement, V3.16
welfare in, V3.6–11, V4.42–7
placement of children in care with parents, V3.45–7
accomodation for child, V3.52
agreement, V3.55
aims and objectives, V3.49
assessment, V3.50–1
breakdown, V3.52
child's views, V3.53–4
consultations, V3.52–3
court directions, V3.48
decision making, V3.54–5
enquiries prior to, V3.51–2
household, V3.59
immediate, V3.47–8
inter-agency arrangements, V3.60
interactions, V3.58
monitoring, V3.56
notification, V3.54–5
outside England and Wales, V3.60–1
overlap of regulations, V3.48
parental responsibility, V3.49
parents who are not carers, V3.55–6
preparation, V3.56
responsible authority, V3.60
short duration, V3.48
short term, V3.48
supervision, V3.56, V3.57–8
Support, V3.51, V3.56–7
termination, V3.59–60
visits, V3.58–9
Placement of Children with Parents etc Regulations (1991), V3.143–9

planning
  basis for decisions, CP.69–73
  and decision making for individual children,
    CP.64–73
  evidence interpretation, CP.72, CP.76
  goals, CP.65
  for individual children, CP.69, CP.75
  objectives, CP.64–5
  perceptual distortions in decision making,
    CP.71–2
  placement, CP.64, CP.65–9
  procedures, V2.79–80
  quality, CP.64
  risk assessment, CP.65–9
  use of statistics, CP.74
  welfare of child, CP.53
planning authority
  range of services for children with
    disabilities, V6.53–4
  in registration of daycare services, V2.50
planning, strategic, CP.54–63
  accurate information for, CP.54–7
  classification, CP.57–9
  evidence for, CP.78
  local authorities, CP.59–62
  policy and guidance, CP.62–3
play
  children's needs, V2.29–30
  sessions, V2.79
playbuses, V2.18
  registration, V2.56
playgroups, V2.16, V2.78
  for children with disabilities, V6.18–19
  extended day, V2.40, V2.78
  peer interactions, V2.38
playworkers, training for, V2.33
pocket money, V4.27–8
police
  accomodation of child, V1.61
  arrest and detention of juveniles, V7.45–6
  in child abuse cases, V4.33
  in child protection work, WT.16–17
  emergency procedures, WT.69
  in emergency protection orders, V6.46
  inter-agency training, WT.17
  investigations and support for child, WT.28
  liaison with local authority, V1.62
  Part V of Act, WT.74–8
  powers, WT.17, V1.60–2
  in registration of daycare services, V2.51
police checks
  on independent visitors, V4.92
  on proposed carers, V3.51
  refuges for children at risk, V4.131, V4.132
Police and Criminal Evidence Act (1984),
  WT.17, V1.49, V7.45
  child protection work, WT.10–11
  detained children, V4.123–4
  search for child, V1.57
police protection, WT.124, V1.60, V1.61
  and contact with chid, V4.67–8
  contact with child, V1.62, V3.64–5
  inter-agency liaison, V1.62
  and parental responsibility, V1.62
  recovery order, V7.31
  responsibilities, V1.61
policy
  effect on practice, CP.62–3
  making, CP.53
  research in development, V2.3
pornography rings, WT.38
Portage Home Teaching scheme, V6.18
portage schemes, V2.17, V6.24
poverty, CP.6

powers of entry, V1.56–7
practical skills and knowledge, V4.108
practice skills, PP.17
pre-birth child protection conference, WT.18,
  WT.49
pregnancy, incidence in care leavers, CP.11
preliminary hearing, WT.124
premises for child care, V2.41–2
premises for private fostering, V8.4
preparation for leaving care, V3.87, V3.91–2
  agencies involved, 100
  Careers Service, V3.106
  counselling, V4.107
  cultural needs, V3.92
  delivery of services, V3.100
  development of self-esteem, V4.107–8
  duty, V3.88
  education, V3.105–6
  family relationships, V3.96–7
  financial assistance provision, V3.101–2
  financial skills, V3.95, V3.98, V4.108
  foster-parents' views, V3.93
  guide to, V3.93
  housing department role, V3.103–4
  independent living skills, V3.91
  interested agencies, V3.92
  involvement of young person, V3.91
  local authority written policies, V3.92–3
  nature of, V3.95–9, V4.105–8
  parental involvement, V3.91
  parents' views, V3.92
  practical skills, V3.95, V3.98, V4.108
  Probation Service role, V3.103
  relationships, V3.91, V3.95, V3.96–7,
    V4.105–6
  schools' role, V3.105–6
  self-esteem, V3.95, V3.97–8
  sexual relationships, V4.107
  social development, V3.91
  social security benefits, V3.107
  specialist services, V3.100
  staff training, V3.100
  support, V3.9,
  training, V3.105–6
  voluntary organisations, V3.102–3
  young people with disabilities, V3.93–5
  young people's views, V3.92
  youth service role, V3.105
  see also after-care; care leavers
primary education
  admission of 4-year olds, V2.44
  availability, V2.65–6
  quantity, V2.65–6
  reception classes, V2.78
primary health care team for disabled young
  people, V6.50–1
principles
  of child care, PP.4–6
  foster placements, PP.16
principles of good child care practice, PP.7–15
  children and their families, PP.7–12
  in relation to agency responsibilities,
    PP.12–15
principles in practice, PP.16–17
  dilemmas, PP.16–17
  hierarchy, PP.16
  implications, PP.17
private law, V1.5
  orders, V2.76
private sector, range of services for children
  with disabilities, V6.53–4
probation officer
  family assistance orders, V2.76
  as guardian ad litem, V7.10

probation order, V4.112
probation service
  in child protection, WT.21
  involvement in after-care, V3.103, V4.112
problem solving, V3.111–12
procedural handbooks see local procedural
  handbooks
prohibited steps order, WT.124, V1.9,
  V1.11–12
  legal framework, WT.70
Prohibition of Female Circumcision Act (1985),
  V8.19
  child protection work, WT.11
prosecution, diversion of juveniles from,
  V1.69–71
protected children, adoption, V9.3
protection of children, V1.44–5
  action with complaints, V4.80
  armed services arrangements, WT.22–3,
    WT.104 6
  of children with disabilities, V6.44–7
  community responsibilities, WT.24
  conference and decision making, WT.31
  day care services, WT.22
  decision making, WT.31
  education service, WT.21–2
  focus of investigation, WT.30
  helpline, WT.23
  investigation of abuse and neglect, WT.9–10
  joint training, WT.53–5
  legal and ethical considerations, WT.9
  no substance in cause for concern, WT.30
  NSPCC, WT.23
  overseas arrangements for Services,
    WT.104–6
  Part V of Act, WT.73–85
  probation service, WT.21
  recording of interviews, WT.30
  records, WT.26
  removal of children from home, WT.10
  understanding of law, WT.2
  voluntary organisations, WT.23
protection from harm, in welfare of child, CP.5
protection order, V1.4
  and contact, V3.64–5, V4.67–8
protection order, emergency, V1.44–5
  and parental responsibility, V2.73–4
psychiatric examination, emergency protection
  orders, V1.59
psychiatric ill health, children in care, CP.8
public liability insurance, V2.36
public, protection of, V4.39
publicising services, V2.13
punishments at independent boarding schools,
  V5.12

Q

questionnaires
  barriers to parental contact, CP.120–3
  behaviour problem analysis, CP.124–9
  for data gathering, CP.89
  distribution of guidance, CP.130–2
  racial and cultural background, CP.106–9
  'Ready to Cope Alone?', CP.90–105
  sibling relationships, CP.110–19

R

Race Relations Act (1976)
  care staff, V4.9
  elimination of racial discrimination, V8.12

racial background
  clothing, V4.27
  questionnaire, CP.106–9
racial groups, day care services, V2.34
racial harassment, foster parents' awareness, V8.9
racial origin
  in placement of children arrangements, V4.43, V4.46–7
  and placement of children in care with parents, V3.51
  in welfare of child, CP.5
reading material, V4.23
'Ready to Cope Alone?', CP.90–105
reception classes, admission of 4-year olds, V2.44
recognisance orders, V1.75
recognition in child protection cases, WT.27
records
  access to, V4.57
  of achievement, V6.15, V6.25
  for child protection work, WT.13
  of complaints, V4.86
  of contact, V4.73
  independent boarding schools, V5.6, V5.20
  inspection of independent boarding schools, V5.19–20, V5.22
  maintenance, PP.14–15
  placement of children arrangements, V3.18, V3.19–21, V4.54, V4.55–7
  protection of children, WT.26
  retention, V4.57
  safekeeping, V4.56
records of children in care
  access, PP.12–13
  confidentiality, PP.12–13
recovery orders, WT.124, V1.64–5, V7.31–2
  expenses, V1.65
  transfer, V7.32
recreation and leisure department, in registration of daycare services, V2.50
referral in child protection cases, WT.27
refuges for children at risk, WT.124, V1.64, V4.130
  acceptance into, V4.131
  applications, V4.130–1
  certificates, V4.130, V4.131
  child in, V1.60
  confidentiality, V4.132
  length of stay, V4.131
  Part V of Act, WT.84–5
  protection from prosecution, V4.130, V4.131
  regulations, V4.130
  short stay, CP.47
  social services department links, V4.132
  voluntary services, V4.112
Refuges (Children's Homes and Foster Placements) Regulations (1991), V4.186–8
register
  of children with disabilities, V6.7–8
  of daycare services, V2.58–9
registered children's homes, V4.143–4
  after-care duties, V3.90–1
  complaints procedures, V6.41
  independent boarding schools as, V5.17
  notification of serious occurrences, WT.36
  representations procedure, V3.108
  restriction of liberty, V4.121
Registered Homes Act (1984), V4.36
Registrar General, V9.3
  Adoption Contact Register, V9.19
  information to counsellor, V9.69
  registers maintained by, V9.72

registration of children's homes, V4.31–2
registration system for day care facilities, V2.26, V2.49–52, V2.49–62
  appeals, V2.61
  applications, V2.51–2, V2.59–60
  cancellation, V2.60–1
  certificate, V2.61
  discretionary requirements, V2.58
  education department, V2.50
  environmental health departments, V2.51
  equipment, V2.56, V2.57
  exemptions, V2.53
  fees, V8.36
  fire department, V2.51
  fit person, V2.54
  follow up, V2.60
  health and safety, V2.51
  inspection, V2.64
  inspection fees, V8.36
  legal department, V2.49–50
  libraries, V2.50
  maintenance and safety, V2.57
  non-parental care of babies and toddlers, V2.56
  occasional, V2.54
  offences, V2.62
  payment of fees, V2.61
  planning department, V2.50
  playbuses, V2.56
  police departments, V2.51
  premises, V2.55–6, V2.57
  publicity, V2.59
  re-registration, V2.62, V8.36
  records, V2.57
  recreation and leisure department, V2.50
  refusal, V2.58
  register, V2.58–9
  requirements, V2.52–3, V2.56–7, V2.58
  staffing, V2.51–2, V2.56–7
  workload of officers, V2.51–2
regulations
  boarding-out, PP.1, PP.3
  focus range and depth, PP.3–6
  in practice, PP.16–17
  status of, PP.2–3
rehabilitation of child, WT.125, V1.37
Rehabilitation of Offenders Act (1974), V4.92
  exceptions, V8.12
Rehabilitation of Offenders Act (1974) (Exceptions) (Amendment) Order (1986), 51
relationships
  building and maintaining, V4.105–6
  family, V3.96–7
  general, V3.96–7
  sexual, V3.97, V4.107
relatives, fostering, CP.27
relief care, CP.51
  scheme, CP.47
religion
  care order placements, V1.36
  for children in homes, V4.2405
  ethos in independent boarding schools, V5.11
  in placement of children arrangements, V4.43, V4.46–7
  and placement of children in care with parents, V3.50
remand, local authority accomodation, V1.75–6, V3.2
remanded children, V4.123–4
remedial service requirements for children in care, CP.34
removal of children from home, WT.10
  emergency by police, WT.78–9

reporting officers, in child protection work, WT.16
reports, pre-sentence, V7.46
Representation Procedure (Children) Regulations (1991), V4.171–7
representation schemes, voluntary organisations, V6.17
representations procedure, V3.108–9, V4.74–5
  actions subsequent to decision, V4.85
  agencies involved, V3.113
  annual report, V4.87
  appropriate procedure, V3.114
  availability of information, V3.112
  for children with disabilities, V6.41–3
  child's involvement, V3.110
  complainants, V4.75–6
  complaints, V3.109–11
  consideration by panel, V4.84–5
  consultation, V4.87
  definitions, V4.75
  eligibility to complain, V3.118, V4.84
  independent element, V3.115–16, V4.81–2
  independent person, V4.84
  information about, V4.78
  involving more than one authority, V3.112–13, V4.78–9
  management, V4.78
  monitoring, V3.120–1, V4.86
  notification of decision, V3.118, V4.84, V4.86
  objectives, V3.111, V4.77
  oral complaints, V4.83
  and other procedures, V4.79
  panel recommendations, V3.119–20
  policy, V3.112
  problem solving, V3.111–12, V4.77
  publicity, V3.112, V4.78
  receipt of complaint, V4.83
  reconsideration of decision, V4.85
  setting up, V3.116–20, V4.82–6
  staffing, V3.115, V4.81
  subjects of complaints, V4.76
  subsequent action, V3.120
  support of those using, V4.80–1
  support in use, V3.114–15
Representations Procedure (Children) Regulations (1991), V3.159–64
Representations Procedure Regulations (1991), transitional arrangements, V7.41
research
  in policy development, V2.3
  underlying issues, CP.77
  use in implementation of Act, CP.7
residence order, WT.125, V1.9–11, V1.17
  as alternative to care and supervision orders, V1.21
  application, V1.13
  discharge of care order, V1.18, V1.33
  with interim supervision order, V1.29
  legal framework, WT.70
  and parental responsibility, V2.73, V6.3
  provision of accomodation, V2.21
  shared, V1.10–11
residential accomodation, V2.1–2
  provision, V3.1
residential care, V4.1
  abuse by staff, WT.34–5
  abuse by visitors, WT.34
  age of children, CP.55
  for children with disabilities, V6.38–40
  classification, CP.59
  complaints, V4.76
  concerns of children, CP.70
  contact arrangements, V4.69

contact with children being looked after, V3.66
extent of use, CP.54–5
investigation of abuse, WT.35–6
isolation, WT.35
meeting needs of young people, CP.55
outside contact opportunities, WT.35
protection in, WT.34–6
publications on, V6.64–5
short-term for children with disabilities, V6.32–3
specialist services, CP.55
success rate, CP.68
for young people with disabilities, V6.51
and young people's needs, CP.74
residential care homes
independent boarding schools as, V5.2
restriction of liberty, V4.121–2
transitional arrangements, V7.43
residential care staff
assumptions about children, CP.70
relationships with social workers, CP.49–50
residential establishment, V2.21
residential placements, V3.1
for family care, V6.34
resources
allocation priorities, V2.2
practical, PP.17
respite care, V3.39, V4.4, V4.41
accomodation provision, CP.21
for children in need, V6.5
development, CP.48
for families of children with disabilities, V6.32–3
family based, CP.21
and fostering, V6.34
medical examination, V6.34
plan of arrangements, V6.34
pre-planned, V6.33–4
publications, V6.64
short-term placements, V6.34
social workers in partnership with parents, CP.47–8
responsible person, WT.125
review of children's cases, WT.125, V3.80–1, V4.58–9
agenda, V3.83, V4.61
attendance, V3.83–4, V4.61–2
chairing, V3.83, V4.61
considerations, V3.84–5
consultation, V3.82–3, V4.60–1
contacts, V3.85
disagreements, V3.87, V4.64
education, V3.85, V3.86
frequency, V3.81, V4.59
health, V3.85
implementing decisions, V3.87, V4.64
independent visitor, V3.85
matters for consideration, V4.62–3
monitoring, V3.87, V4.64
notification, V4.63–4
parents in, V4.61, V4.62, V4.63
plan, V4.62
and planning process, V4.60
preparations for, V4.60
report, V3.85–6, V4.63
requirement, V3.81, V4.59
short-term placements, V3.81
system, V3.81–6, V4.59–64
transitional arrangements, V7.40–1
venue, V3.84, V4.62
welfare plan for child, V3.84
Review of Children's Cases Regulations (1991), V1.33–4, V3.72, V3.154–8, V4.163–8

health considerations, V4.167
schedules, V4.166–7
review regulations, transitional arrangements for children in care, V7.37
rewards at independent boarding schools, V5.12
rights
of children, V2.37
of parents, V2.38
of workers with young children, V2.38
risk, children at, V4.130
assessment, WT.2–3
compulsory intervention, V1.4
Royal Air Force, child protection, WT.105
Royal Marines, child protection, WT.105
Royal Navy, child protection, WT.105
rules and regulations, Part V of Act, WT.85
Rumbold Report, V2.29, V2.30
runaway youngsters, refuges, V4.130

S

safe houses, WT.124
see also refuges
sanctions
at independent boarding schools, V5.12
in children's homes, V4.17
sanitary accomodation at independent boarding schools, V5.9
sanitary requisites, V4.28
school
admission of children from overseas, V8.28–9
careers guidance, V3.105–6
change under education supervision orders, V7.26–7
health education, WT.22
involvement in education supervision orders, V7.25
non-attendance, V1.63, V6.25–6
non-maintained special, V4.4, V4.32
poor attendance pattern, V7.23
psychological services, V6.24
return to for unqualified young people, V3.106
role in after-care, V4.115
role in preparation for leaving care, V3.105–6
trips, V1.7
under-expectation of young people in care, V3.105
vetting staff, V4.8–9
school age children
in day care, V2.33
need for services, V2.29
School Health Service, V5.9, V8.17
School Medical Officer, V5.9, V5.10
searching for children, V1.56–7
Secretary of State, inspection powers of independent boarding schools, V5.18
section 8 orders, WT.125, V1.9–13
adoption proceedings, V1.18
applications for, V1.13–15
with child assessment orders, V1.49
child's application, V1.14
discharge by care orders, V1.36
with family assistance orders, V1.16
foster parents, V1.14
grandparents, V1.14
interim, V1.29
local authority, V1.14–15
making by courts, V1.18

older children, V1.15
types, V1.9–12
secure accomodation, V1.4, V4.118
access to professional support, V4.119
avoidance of need, V4.119
for children with disabilities, V6.38–9
independent visitor, V4.95
for juvenile remands, V7.46
maximum period, V4.121, V4.126
minimum age, V4.122
notifications, V4.124
in plan for child's welfare, V4.119
records, V4.129
regulations, V4.180–5
reviews, V4.128–9
transitional arrangements for children in care, V7.37
use of placements, V4.118
secure accomodation application
courts powers in, V4.120–7
and GALRO service, V7.4
of regulations, V4.121
to court, V1.67–8, V4.121
to High Court, V4.128
secure accomodation orders, V1.66, V7.33–4
appeals, V1.68
court powers, V1.67–8
court's role, V1.67
criteria for restriction of liberty, V1.66–7
duration, V1.67
juveniles remanded to local authority accomodation, V1.66–7, V1.68
legal representation, V1.67
Secure Accomodation Regulations, V1.66
secure order, V4.119
security, and permanence, CP.23
self confidence of child in care, PP.10–11
self-esteem, development, V3.97–8, V4.107–8
semi-independent living, V2.21
separation, parental responsibility, V2.74
service planning, PP.13
for individual child, V2.7
sex education, V4.107
sexual abuse, 46, WT.49, V3.97
remedial service requirements of children, CP.34
removal of alleged abuser, V1.52
supervised contact, V1.59
sexual development, young people with disabilities, V6.52
Sexual Offences Act (1956), V7.35
sexuality, V3.97
sexually abused children, foster parents, V3.31
SHAC, V4.112
Shelter, V3.103, V4.112
sheltered housing
for after-care, V4.113, V4.114
voluntary services, V4.112
shopping, V4.27
for food, V4.26
short-term placements, V3.81
sibling relationships, CP.27–33
breakdown of placements, CP.30
in care placements, CP.36–7
check list analysis and interpretation, CP.111
permanent placements, CP.29, CP.30
questionnaires, CP.110–19
separation, CP.28, CP.29
step-siblings, CP.30–3
siblings
accomodated together, V4.39
care, PP.9
in placement of children arrangements, V4.42

and placement of children in care with parents, V3.51

sickle cell anaemia, V4.20, V4.44
accomodation suitability for privately fostered children, V8.8

sign language, V6.32

single parent families, CP.6–7, V2.30

SKILL, V6.50

sleep deprivation, V4.19

sleeping rough, V3.104, V4.114

social deviance, children in care, CP.8

social enquiry report, for residence requirement in criminal supervision orders, V1.74

social networks, CP.34

social order, powers of entry, V1.56

social security benefits, V4.117
for children with disabilities, V6.58–9
claims procedure, V4.24
for contact with children being looked after, V3.67
for young people leaving care, V3.107
see also child benefit

Social Services, joint sub-committee with Education Authority, V2.77

social services department
after-care responsibilities, V3.99
after-care services for young people with disabilities, V4.103–5
assessment of needs before leaving school, V6.49
assessment procedures for children in need, V6.9
care management planning, V6.10
chairing child protection conference, WT.46
child abuse at independent boarding schools, V5.6
in child abuse cases, V4.33
child protection register, WT.47
in child protection work, WT.15–16
co-operation with DHAs for children with disabilities, V6.28
collaboration with housing authorities, V2.20
complaints procedures, CP.46, V6.41, V6.42
complaints records at independent boarding schools, V5.13
contact from public, WT.16
counselling of abused children, V5.6
day care for children in need, V6.5
day care review duties, V6.20
duties with education supervision orders, V7.28
in education supervision orders, V7.23
facilitation of provision of support services, V6.16
family centres, V6.18–19
family support, V2.8
frequency of visits to independent boarding schools, V5.14
functions in relation to children with disabilities, V6.1
guide to after-care services, V4.103
identification of children in need, V6.6
inspection of independent boarding schools, V5.2, V5.3, V5.14
inspection of premises, V5.20–1
inspection of private fostering, V6.37
investigation of abuse and neglect, WT.9–10
LEA involvement, V6.21–6
legal responsibilities, WT.9
liaison with child health services, V6.27
liaison with education department, V4.104, V4.105
links with refuges for children at risk, V4.132

looking after children with disabilities, V6.31
notification of accomodation of children with disabilities, V6.39–40
notification by LEA of special educational needs, V6.22–3
packages of support, V6.10
parental responsibility acquisition, V6.3
placement of children in independent boarding schools, V5.15–16
plan for children with disabilities, V6.13
policy on leaving care, V4.102
practice guide for care management and assessment, V6.12
private fostering notification, V8.16–17
provision of services for children with disabilities, V6.2, V6.53
publicising services to children in need, V6.6
record inspection at independent boarding schools, V5.6
records of staff at independent boarding schools, V5.7
responsibilities after leaving care, V4.109
role in after-care, V3.88
services for children in need, V6.5–6
staff liaison in independent boarding schools, V5.4
support of child leaving care, V4.97–8
visits to independent boarding schools, V5.8, V5.14–15
written policies for leaving care, V3.92–3

Social Services Inspectorate, V4.4

social work qualification for supervisor of education supervision orders, V7.24

Social Work (Scotland) Act (1968), V8.3

social worker
in access disputes, CP.42
assessment of foster parent applicants, V3.25
child's wishes in private fostering, V8.10–11
code of ethics, WT.12
and foster parents, V3.31, V3.32, V8.9–10
as guardians ad litem, V7.10
helpful qualities, CP.47
hospital, V6.29, V6.40
implications of Children Act, CP.1
inter-agency training, WT.17
links between family and child in care, CP.25–7
needs of child for placement, V3.15
parents' agent role, CP.51
partnership with parents, CP.39
policy confusion, CP.63
post qualifying training, WT.54
predictions of problems with placements, CP.71
principles of child care, PP.6
relationship with child in foster care, V3.37
relationships with foster carers and residential staff, CP.49–50
respite care schemes, CP.47–8
scientific discipline, CP.78
suitability of foster parent, V8.11, V8.12
supporting home on trial placements, CP.47
termination of placement of child in care with parents, V3.59
training foster parents, V3.31
understanding of child's wishes, V3.67
use of evidence, CP.77 8
visits to children in care with parents, V3.58–9

Soldiers, Sailors and Airmens Families Association (SSAFA), V3.40

space standards for child care, V2.41–2

special educational needs, V2.33–4

advice required, V6.22
assessment, WT.118, V6.21–2, V6.25, V6.28
early identification, V6.23–4
foster parents' support, V8.13
integration, V6.25
minority ethnic groups, V6.65
non-attendance at school, V6.26
notification to SSDs, V6.22–3
parental involvement in assessment, V6.23
publications, V6.62–3
reviews of statements, V6.23
special circumstances, V6.22
statement of, V3.10, V3.94, V4.46, V4.104, V6.22, V6.25
under fives, V6.23–4
young people over 16, V6.26

special needs
contact with parents, V1.39
foster parents for, V3.25
special schools, V3.70
non-maintained, V5.2, V5.17

specific issue order, WT.126, V1.9, V1.12
legal framework, WT.70

stability of care, V2.39

staff
AIDS awareness, V4.20–1
allocation of responsibility, V4.11–12
of children's homes, V4.7–8
contacts with teachers, V4.22
group composition, V4.9
handbook, V5.5
hygiene training, V4.27
inappropriate conduct, V4.30
induction, V5.3
information about complaints, V4.81
for interviewing in child protection investigations, WT.29
meetings in children's homes, V4.11
office space in children's homes, V4.13
reports for court, V4.125
representations procedure, V4.78
in residential settings and suspicion of abuse, WT.35
selection, V4.9
supervision, V5.5
supervision in children's homes, V4.10–11
support, V4.9
support in caring for vulnerable children, V6.29
support in complaints procedure, V3.115
understanding of assumptions of Act, WT.2
vetting, V4.8–9
written guidance for children's homes, V4.9–10

staff at independent boarding schools, V5.5
awareness of child abuse, V5.6
checks on, V5.7–8, V5.20
complaints procedure, V5.13
disciplinary measures in child abuse cases, V5.7
references, V5.8
training needs, V5.6

staff/child ratios
for child care, V2.41, V2.43
childminding, V2.45
day care services for school age children, V2.47
for nursery education, V2.44

statement, V4.46
of policy on leaving care, V3.92–3
see also special educational needs, statement of

States Children Board (Guernsey), V7.31

statistics
  reliability, CP.74
  use in planning, CP.54
statutory checklist, V1.17
Statutory Instruments
  Contact with Children Regulations,
    V3.150–1
  Foster Placement Regulations, V3.131–42
  Independent Visitors, V3.152–3
  Placement of Children with Parents
    Regulations, V3.143–9
  Placement of Children Regulations,
    V3.122–30
  Representations Procedure, V3.159–64
  Review of Cases, V3.154–8
step-siblings, CP.30–3
  ages, CP.30–2
stress
  children experiencing from peers, CP.32
  from peers in care, CP.32, CP.37
supervised activities, V2.17, V2.46, V2.79
supervising officer for education supervision
  orders, V7.24, V7.25–6
  directions use, V7.27, V7.28
supervision, with residence requirement, V3.2
supervision order, WT.126, V1.20, V1.39–42,
  V4.112
  age of child, 23
  appeals against, V1.34–5
  applications for, V1.21–7
  breach of requirement or direction, V1.41
  child's consent to examination and
    assessment, V1.40
  conditions for, V1.23–6
  considerations in applications, V1.21–3
  court requirements, V1.26–7
  in criminal proceedings, V1.42, V1.72–5
  criteria for, WT.26
  discharge, V1.20, V1.33–4
  duration, V1.41
  duties of supervisor, V1.39–40
  and education supervision orders, V7.28
  extension, V7.46
  harm to child, V1.23–4
  legal framework, WT.66–7
  medical and psychiatric examination of child,
    V1.40–1
  order making powers, V1.21
  parental responsibility in, V1.40
  party status, V1.26–7
  repeat applications, V1.34
  threshold criteria, V1.24
  timetable, V1.27
  transitional arrangements, V1.80, V7.42
  treatment, V1.41
  under Children and Young Persons Act
    (1969), V1.21, V1.23
  variation, V1.20, V1.33–4
supervision order, interim order, V1.27,
  V1.28–33, V1.29–30
  assessment of child, V1.28, V1.29,
    V1.30–2
  child's consent to examination or
    assessment, V1.31–2
  criteria, V1.28
  duration, V1.28
  effects, V1.32–3
  medical and psychiatric assessment, V1.28,
    V1.29, V1.30–2
  with residence order, V1.29
  responsibilities arising from, V1.32–3
supervision proceedings, welfare principle
  application, V1.2
supervision sessions for staff, V4.10–11

supervisor
  discharge or variation of orders, V1.33,
    V1.34
  duties, V1.39–40
support
  networks for young people with disabilities,
    V6.52
  ongoing for children with disabilities,
    V6.48–9
Supreme Court Act (1981), V1.34
surveillance of child health, V6.27

T

teaching service, peripatetic, V6.24
telephone
  access to in residential settings, WT.35
  at independent boarding schools, V5.11
terminal illness, V6.28
  accomodation for children, V6.39
  publications on care of children, V6.63
termination of access, local authorities, CP.61
terminology, PP.1–2
thalassaemia, V4.20, V4.44
  accomodation suitability for privately
    fostered children, V8.8
timetables, WT.126
toddlers, daycare, V2.56
toy libraries, V2.18, V6.19
training
  and after-care, V4.115–16
  children's home staff, V4.7–8
  communication with children with disabilities,
    V6.15
  expenses, V3.89
  financial assistance, V4.111
  financial assistance from local authority,
    V3.101
  grant, V4.99
  help in obtaining, V4.23
  inter-agency, WT.54
  local authority assistance, V3.106–7
  materials, WT.55
  preparation for leaving care, V3.105–6
  for voluntary sector, V6.17
  for young people with disabilities, V6.50
training, joint
  for child protection workers, WT.53–5
  development of opportunities, WT.54–5
  non-professional staff, WT.54
  programmes, WT.53–4
  provision for, WT.54–5
training, multi-disciplinary, WT.23
transitional arrangements, V4.100, V7.35–44
  boarded-out children, V7.39
  childminders, V7.43
  children in care, V7.36–8
  criminal care orders, V7.44
  criminal supervision orders, V7.42
  directions and injunctions, V7.38
  for emigration of children in care, V7.41
  fostering limit, V7.43
  independent boarding schools, V7.43–4
  LEA accomodation, V7.43
  liability to contribute, V7.41
  for maintenance contributions by local
    authorities, V7.41
  mental nursing homes, V7.43
  nurseries, V7.43
  nursing homes, V7.43
  place of safety orders, V7.42
  placement with parents, V7.39
  private children's homes, V7.42

  private fostering, V7.43
  Representations Procedure Regulations
    (1991), V7.41
  residential care homes, V7.43
  reviews of children's cases, V7.40–1
  supervision orders, V7.42
  voluntary care, V7.39
  wardship proceedings, V7.38
transport authority, range of services for
  children with disabilities, V6.53–4
Travellers' families, V6.17
trust, relationship of child with independent
  visitor, V4.94

U

under fives
  adult-child interaction, V2.38
  needs for services, V2.29
  quality of care, V2.36–40
under fives education
  food, V2.42
  furniture and equipment, V2.42
  group sizes, V2.42
  happiness of children, V2.40
  health and safety conditions, V2.39
  interpersonal relationships, V2.39
  learning opportunities, V2.39
  observation, V2.42
  peer interactions, V2.38–9
  premises, V2.41–2
  provision, V2.32–3
  quality of care, V2.40
  records, V2.42
  space standards, V2.41–2
  stability of care, V2.39
  staff/child ratios, V2.41
  standards, V2.40–5
  toys, V2.42
  unit sizes, V2.42
under-expectation by schools, V4.115
United States Air Force, child protection,
  WT.106
unruliness, certificate of, V1.76
upbringing, standard of, V1.25
usual fostering limit, V3.110
  appeals against, V4.79
  see also fostering limit

V

video recording, WT.30
views of child, V2.75
visitors
  contact with at independent boarding
    schools, V5.10
  independent see independent visitor
visits
  independent visitor, V4.93–4
  restrictions, V4.18, V8.13
  to children's homes by responsible
    authorities, V4.31
vocational training for young people with
  disabilities, V6.49, V6.52
Voice for the Child in Care, V4.128
voluntary agreement, child looked after by,
  contact with child, V4.66
voluntary care, transitional arrangements,
  V7.39
voluntary homes, V3.70
  notification of particulars, V4.144
  registration, V4.31, V4.143

restriction of liberty, V4.121
voluntary organisations
  accomodation of children, V5.17
  after-care duties, V3.90, V4.100
  day care services, V2.27
  employees as guardians ad litem, V7.10
  foster placements, V3.43–4
  information for parents of children in need,
    V6.23
  local groups, V6.19
  in planning local services, V6.16
  range of services for children with
    disabilities, V6.53–4
  representation schemes, V6.17
  representations procedure, V3.108
  review of children accomodated by, V4.38
  service provision, V6.16–17
  SSDs in provision of support, V6.16
voluntary sector aftercare services, V3.102
volunteers, local authority responsibilities,
  V2.27–8
vulnerability, consideration of, PP.7
vulnerable children, responsibilities of agencies
  to, PP.14, PP.15

W

ward of court, WT.126
wardship, V1.12, V1.42, V2.75
  and inherent jurisdiction of High Court,
    V4.127–8
wardship proceedings, V4.131, V7.35
  children in care, V7.36
welfare
  of children in independent boarding schools,
    V5.17–18

of children looked after by local authority,
  V4.38–9
consideration of court, WT.63
contribution of restriction of liberty, V4.127,
  V4.128
duty of local authorities, V2.5
independent visitor's role, V4.93
interests of child in making secure order,
  V4.120
long-term, PP.12
parents' needs and wishes, 45
in placement of children arrangements,
  V4.42–7
planning placement of children
  arrangements, V4.42
relevant factors, CP.5
report, WT.126
responsibilities of local authorities, V2.3
services for young people with disabilities,
  V3.94
significance of non-production, V1.49
welfare of child, promotion, CP.5, CP.19–23
  care and supervision orders, V1.20
  family links, CP.24–7
  implications for policy and practice, CP.34–7
  meeting needs and developing potential,
    CP.6–17
  sibling relationships, CP.27–33
  young people moving into independence,
    CP.9–13
welfare principle
  child-centred, V1.1–2
  delay, V1.17
  in making orders, V1.17
  need for continuity, PP.4
  statement, PP.5
wishes of child, V2.75
witnesses
  children as, V7.45

interviewing children, WT.53
women, working, V2.30
workers
  counselling, V2.23
  rights, V2.38
  support services, V2.22–3
Working Together, 3, PP.1
Working with Under Sevens project, V2.33
written agreements, CP.43, WT.126
  in fostering, CP.49
  in partnership work, CP.51

Y

young offenders *see* juvenile offenders
young people
  continuing needs, V3.99
  views on preparation for leaving care, V3.93
young people leaving care
  agencies involved, V4.110
  delivery of services, V4.110
  financial assistance, V4.110–11
  preparation, V4.97
  specialist services, V4.110
  voluntary sector role, V4.112
youth clubs, V3.24
youth court, V7.47
youth service
  aftercare role, V3.99, V4.109, V4.114–15
  disabled young people's needs, V3.105
  role in preparation for leaving care, V3.105
Youth Training (YT), V3.106, V3.107, V4.116
  and income support, V4.117
Youth Treatment Centre, V3.70, V4.120
  applications to court for secure
    accomodation, V4.125

LIST OF PUBLICATIONS ON THE CHILDREN ACT

I Regulations and Guidance

Name of Publication	Date of Issue/ Launch	ISBN No. or Reference No.
An introduction to the Children Act 1989	November 1989	0 11 321254 2
Volume 1—Court Orders	March 1991	0 11 321371 9
Volume 2—Family Support, Day Care and Educational Provision for Young Children	March 1991	0 11 321372 7
Volume 3—Family Placements	April 1991	0 11 321375 1
Volume 4—Residential Care	July 1991	0 11 321430 8
Volume 5—Independent Schools	April 1991	0 11 321373 5
Volume 6—Children with Disabilities	September 1991	0 11 321452 9
Volume 7—Guardians Ad Litem and other Court Related Issues	October 1991	0 11 321471 5
Volume 8—Private Fostering and Miscellaneous	October 1991	0 11 321473 1
Volume 9—Adoption Issues	October 1991	0 11 321474 X
Patterns and Outcomes in Child Placement	May 1991	0 11 321357 3
Working Together under the Children Act 1989: A guide to arrangements for Inter-Agency Co-operation for the Protection of Children from Abuse (New edition)	October 1991	0 11 321472 3
The Welfare of Children in Boarding Schools Practice Guide	October 1991	0 11 321477 4
Registration of Childminding and Day care: Using the Law to Improve Standards	October 1991	0 11 321469 3
Practice Guide for GALROs	July 1992	0 11 321495 2
Guidance for GALRO Panel Managers	July 1992	0 11 321505 3
Timetabling of Care Proceedings before the implementation of the Children Act 1989	February 1992	0 11 321487 1
The Care of Children—Principles and Practice in Regulations and Guidance	1989	0 11 321289 5
Looking After Children—Assessing Outcomes in Child Care	December 1991	0 11 321459 6
The Children Act 1989: What every Nurse, Health Visitor and Midwife needs to know	March 1992	COI/HSSH J1548NJ O/N 19207
An Introductory Guide to the NHS	September 1991	COI/HSSH J1403NJ O/N 16050
Child protection: Guidance for Senior Nurses, Health Visitors and Midwives (Second edition 1992)	1992	0 11 321501 0

Name of Publication	Date of Issue/ Launch	ISBN No. or Reference No.
Guidance on completion of statistical returns	Generally included with the relevant return	—

II Training Materials

Name of Publication	Date of Launch/ Issue	ISBN No. or Reference No.
National Children's Bureau Children and Group Day care, aimed principally at those responsible for registration and inspection in SSDs	16 May 1991 Launched by Minister of Health	Participant's pack 0 90 281766 3 Trainers' pack 0 90 281767 1
National Children's Bureau Child Protection Training Project designed principally for local authority staff in relation to court orders obtainable for the protection of children	1 May 1991 Launched by Minister of Health	0 90 281762 0
Family Rights Group Working in Partnership with Children and Families and Communities. It aims to give social workers and their managers a thorough knowledge of the inter-relationship of law and practice in relation to partnership and prevention	24 July 1991 Launched by P.S.S. Health	0 11 321447 2

III Training and Materials Centrally Commissioned

Name and Description of Pack and Preparing Body	Date of Launch	ISBN No. or Reference No.
Open University "Putting it into Practice" Deals with the overall philosophy of the Children Act prepared jointly Department of Health with LCD Principally for social workers, local authority lawyers and magistrates	23 January 1991 Launched by Minister of Health 29 January 1991 Launched by Lord Chancellor	0 74 924348 1 —
Additional material for Chairmen of Family Proceedings Courts	May 1991	—
Training pack for NHS Professionals	August 1992	0 11 321518 5
P558: The Children Act: Court Order Cards 1–23 in Braille	December 1991	—
Leicester University Children In Need and their Families: A New Approach. A guide to Part III of the Act for local authority managers	November 1990	0 9511996 1 7

Name and Description of Pack and Preparing Body	Date of Launch	ISBN No. or Reference No.
Manual for Senior Managers of SSDs. Deals with the philosophy of the Act and major changes it brings about	May 1991	—
The Children Act—An Advisors Guide (video)	July 1991	—
University of East Anglia Training materials on Parental and Older Child Involvement in Child Protection Work	September 1992	—
Parentline Map of the Act	June 1992	0 9519430 0 6

IV   Children Act Publicity—Leaflets etc

Name of Publication	Date of Launch	ISBN No. or Reference No.
To date six booklets and a leaflet have been issued on the Children Act:		
The Children Act and the Courts—A Guide for Parents	1991	CAG2
The Children Act and Local Authorities—A Guide for Parents	1991	CAG1
The Children Act and You—A Guide for Young People (leaflet)	1991	CAG3
The Children Act and the Courts—A Guide for Children and Young People	1992	CAG6
Getting Help from the Social Services—A Guide for Children and Young People	1992	CAG5
Living Away from Home Your Rights—A Guide for Children and Young People	1992	CAG7
Children Act and Day Care—A Guide to the Law	1991	CAG4
Family Rights Group Child Protection Procedures—What they mean for your family	July 1992	—
Stepfamily A Step in Both Directions? The Impact of the Children Act 1989 on Stepfamilies	February 1992	1873309066

LIST OF ERRATA AND ADDENDA TO CHILDREN ACT GUIDANCE AND REGULATIONS.

1 **Volume 2** **Family Support, Day Care and Educational Provision for Young Children**

i *Annex D, Section D*

Add to paragraph 1 (Legislation):

"The Control of Substances Hazardous to Health Regulations, 1988

"Households will often have several substances hazardous to children. These regulations apply to the control of such substances."

ii **Amend paragraph 2: Health and Safety Requirements – Domestic Premises to read:**

"2. The Health and Safety at Work Act places general duties on all people at work to ensure that their work activity does not affect health and safety of others. It applies to employers, employees, the self-employed, those in control of premises and anyone else connected with work activity. For employers, the two most important duties are to ensure, so far as reasonably practicable, the health, safety and welfare of their employees (s.2) and to protect third parties against risks to their health and safety arising from their work activities (s.3). For self-employed childminders, its most important effect is to lay a duty on them to ensure their work does not affect the health and safety of the children in their care or of others."

iii **Add to paragraph 6:**

"A publication on health and safety designed specifically for small businesses is The Essentials of Health and Safety at Work available from HMSO."

iv *Bibliography* (page 69–70)

Add to Codes of Practice:

"**A Good Practice Guide**. National Playbus Association."

2 **Volume 3** **Family Placements**

Errors in the Regulations printed as Annexes in Volume 3: Family Placements

There are a number of printer's errors in Annexes to Volume 3 which reproduces various sets of regulations 1991 made under the Children Act. Local authorities should note that the corrections in paragraphs ii(e) and iii(a) below are the most significant. The errors are as follows:

i **Arrangements for Placement of Children (General) Regulations 1991 (SI 1991/890)**

(a) Page 122: under "Schedules", in "1. Considerations to which..." *insert* "are" before "to have regard".

(b) Page 125: insert "(1)" after "7" (Health requirements).

(c)   Page 128: in title of Schedule 3 *insert* "to which responsible authorities are to have regard".

(d)   Page 129: in paragraph 5 of Schedule 4, *insert* "with respect to the child" after "decision making". In paragraph 7 insert "for contact" after "arrangements".

ii   Foster Placement (Children) Regulations 1991 (SI 1991/910)

(a)   Page 132: in Regulation 1(3) insert "any such notice" after "in writing and".

(b)   Page 133: in Regulation 2(3) insert "on" after "(whether before...".

(c)   Page 134: in the third line of Regulation 6(1) replace "this" by "that".

(d)   Page 135: in Regulation 7(2) insert "area" before "authority" in the third line.

(e)   *Page 137: in Regulation 11 insert at the end "(5) Where a local authority make a placement under this regulation outside their area they shall notify the area authority." In Regulation 13(3) delete "a copy of each".*

(f)   Page 140: in paragraph 1 of Schedule 2 insert "amount of" before "support".

(g)   Page 140: Annotation to "Schedule 3" heading should read "Regulation 5(6)" not Regulation 5(5)

(h)   Page 141: in paragraph 6 of Schedule 3 replace "under" with "order".

iii   Contact with Children Regulations 1991 (SI 1991/891)

(a)   Page 150: delete second Regulation 1(3).

iv   Review of Children's Cases Regulations 1991 (SI 1991/895)

(a)   Page 154: in paragraph 2 of the list of Schedules replace "local" with "responsible".

3   Volume 4   Residential Care

i   Para 1.174, 4 and 5 lines from the end "Sch 14 Para 2" *should read* "Schedule 14 Para 32(2)".

4   Volume 7   Guardians ad Litem and other Court related issues

Chapter 2

paragraph 2.89 line 1: "Paragraph 2.39" *should read* "Paragraph 2.58".

Chapter 6

paragraph 6.9 line 3: After "custodianship orders are deemed to" delete "be parental responsibility orders" and insert "confer parental responsibility on the holder of the order for as long as the order lasts".

paragraph 6.16 line 4: delete words "freeing for adoption or".

paragraph 6.43 line 8: After "it will run for a year from" delete words "14 October 1991" and insert "the date the original order was made".

5 Volume 8 Private Fostering and Miscellaneous

There are a number of Printer's errors in this volume:

i   *page 8, paragraph 1.4.21* 3rd line "particular attention should be given..."

ii *page 33, paragraph 2.7* "– type of offence or order", "– the degree of culpability of the person".

6 Volume 9 Adoption issues

i   *page v Contents* Section 1 – delete bold A, B, C and D.

ii *page 3, paragraph 1.22* "The Register will only be open to people...".

7 Working together under the Children Act 1989: A guide to arrangements for inter-agency co-operation for the protection of children from abuse

i   Page 6: in paragraph 2.12(b) *replace* "legal" with "local".

ii   Page 33: in paragraph 5.18.1, line 5 *replace* "minimum" with "maximum".

iii Page 41: in paragraph 6.1, line 2 *replace* "chld" with "child"

iv   Page 35: paragraph 5.20.11, line 2 "paras 1.888–1.889 *should read* "1.188–1.189"

Printed in the United Kingdom for HMSO
Dd295502 C270 11/92 G531/2 10170